The Origins of *Culture and Anarchy*

FRED G. WALCOTT

The Origins of

CULTURE

&

ANARCHY

Matthew Arnold & Popular Education in England

UNIVERSITY OF TORONTO PRESS

© University of Toronto Press 1970
Printed in Canada by University of Toronto Press
Toronto and Buffalo
ISBN 0-8020-5229-0

Published in Great Britain by
Heinemann Educational Books Ltd.
London and Edinburgh

Quotations on
pages 8 and 92 from
G. A. N. Lowndes,
The Silent Social Revolution
(London, 1937),
p. 13 and p. 11, and
on pages 31 and 34 from
Howard Foster Lowry,
*The Letters of Matthew Arnold
to Arthur Hugh Clough*
(London and New York, 1932),
p. 68 ff and pp. 68–9,
by permission of
the Clarendon Press, Oxford.

CONTENTS

FOREWORD

"For the creation of a master-work of literature two powers must concur, the power of the man and the power of the moment, and the man is not enough without the moment; the creative power has, for its happy exercise, appointed elements, and those elements are not in its own control." This is no doubt the best known of Arnold's many expressions of his sense that every man is moulded, in ways he cannot avoid, by the age into which he is born; that he is the product of his character and of the character of his age.

In very many ways, Arnold's own character and career were entirely predictable, given his inheritance. His intellectual bent he certainly took from his father; it was inevitable that he should be a classicist and that he should be fundamentally concerned with problems of church and religion. If Dr. Arnold was no poet, his influence showed itself even in his son's principal avocation: "Mycerinus" was set as subject of a Rugby prize poem not long after Dr. Arnold assumed the head-master-ship, and the concluding images of two of Matthew Arnold's best-known poems, "The Scholar-Gipsy" and "Dover Beach," were drawn from the great historian whom Dr. Arnold edited and to whom both father and son were devoted, Thucydides. Matthew Arnold should have become, like his father, a schoolmaster, a university professor, ultimately (as one feels his father must certainly have become) a dean or a bishop.

But it was precisely there that the spirit of the age intervened. An academic career was ordinarily open, in Matthew Arnold's day as in his father's, only to the clergy, and in the son's view the time had gone by when a man of ideas could take orders: "[Papa] is the last free speaker of the Church of England clergy who speaks without being shackled, and without being obviously aware that he is so, and that he is in a false position in consequence; and the moment a writer feels this his power is gone. I may add, that if a clergyman does not feel this now, he ought to feel it. The best of them (Jowett, for example) obviously do feel it, and I am quite sure Papa would have felt it had he been living now, and thirty years younger. Not that he would have been less a Christian, or less zealous for a national Church, but his attention would have been painfully awake to the truth that to profess to see Christianity through the spectacles of a number of second or third-rate men who lived in Queen Elizabeth's time (and this is what office-holders under the Thirty-Nine Articles do) – men whose works one never dreams of reading for the purpose of enlightening and edifying oneself – is an intolerable absurdity, and that it is time to put the formularies of the Church of England on a solider basis." And so, after a few years as Fellow of Oriel College, Arnold sought his vocation elsewhere.

The age provided the alternative. When Arnold was ten years old, Parliament for the first time granted assistance for the building of schools, and the schools that received assistance were obliged to be inspected. Eighteen years later Arnold became one of Her Majesty's lay inspectors of schools. His motive was ostensibly merely to have a fixed income upon which to marry; his early letters, written with a young man's superciliousness, betray at best mere tolerance of his arduous tasks. But as the government moved more and more inevitably to the assumption of responsibility for the education of the people, Arnold found himself carried on the tide of the future: here was a sphere of operation for an educator that required all the energy and intelligence Dr. Thomas Arnold had poured into the public-school mould, but without the clericalism, and indeed with a stronger assurance that this was where the future lay. One of Matthew's brothers, Edward, also became a lay inspector; even Clough, for whom the older pattern of teaching almost had been disastrous, found his final home in the Education Department.

And because of this shift in the pattern of an educator's career, Matthew Arnold was placed in constant contact with people he might otherwise hardly have known the existence of – not merely the middle class, but the lower classes. The poverty of the East End of London was visible whenever his inspectoral rounds took him there. If he didn't know the workers, he knew their children, and he watched the financial struggles of some of them as they grew up to be teachers themselves. The consequence was a strong practical concern for the social condition of England, a concern based both on the Oxford ideal and on the practical observation of a man who could see with his own eyes what that condition was. *Culture and Anarchy* is both the fruit of this observation and the type of this disposition: its first chapter, later called "Sweetness and Light," was a lecture from the Chair of Poetry at Oxford, but its last chapter contains some of the most eloquent and clear-sighted remarks on the effect of industrial laissez-faire upon the people of England which the age of the second Reform Law produced.

Almost every aspect of Matthew Arnold's work, then, was in some measure predictable from his heritage. But one aspect was not: the social concern that produced *Culture and Anarchy* was owing to the "power of the moment" – the moment, that is, that required an intelligent educator to see his future not in the Church and the schools of the past, but in the Education Department and the schools of the future. It is Professor Walcott's clear perception of the relation between the school inspector and the author of *Culture and Anarchy* that makes his book original and significant.

R. H. SUPER

INTRODUCTION

Matthew Arnold became an inspector of elementary schools in 1851. At the time, he was already a poet, though but little known. His first thin book, *The Strayed Reveller, and Other Poems*, had appeared in 1849 under the anonymous authorship of "A." A second volume, *Empedocles on Etna, and Other Poems*, was published three years later (1852) under the same designation. Not until 1853 did his full name grace a volume. This book was entitled simply *Poems by Matthew Arnold*. The 1853 edition, however, bore a substantial Preface, explaining in terms of classical criticism his reasons for substituting "Sohrab and Rustum" for the "Empedocles on Etna" in the earlier collection. This Preface, reprinted in the *Poems* of 1854, revealed an admirable acquaintance with ancient literature and ancient critical theory. At the end of 1857, *Merope*, a tragedy after the Sophoclean manner, appeared bearing also an elaborate critical introduction. The erudition shown in these prefatory essays is impressive; and this, together with the earlier obscurity, makes significant the statement of Sir Arthur T. Quiller-Couch, "that the most and the best of Arnold's poetry was written before he gained the world's ear, and that he gained it not as a poet but as a critic."[1]

In May of 1857, Arnold was elected to the Chair of Poetry at Oxford, whereupon his stature as a critic was soon augmented. The lectures *On Translating Homer* and the *Essays in Criticism*, First Series, were given from this eminence. Such are the familiar facts that impressed the literary world and established Arnold's scholarly reputation.

Meanwhile, with his appointment as Her Majesty's Inspector of

1 *The Poems of Matthew Arnold, 1840–1867* (London, 1930), p. vi.

Schools, quite another side of his life had its beginning – a plodding, dull routine entailing its full measure of drudgery and frustration. For thirty-five years Arnold was to bear this onerous burden, a phase of his active life holding little attraction for the devotee of letters. The ends of such toil are official reports, with their prosaic facts and figures. But in Arnold's case there are many close relationships between the literary side and that devoted to his nation's schools. He himself considered several of his official reports on foreign schools as worthy of publication, and he thus offered them to the world. His *Popular Education of France* came in 1861 and *Schools and Universities on the Continent* followed in 1868. Six years later he re-published from the latter work the nine chapters on Germany under the title of *Higher Schools and Universities in Germany* (1874).

The value of Arnold's official papers greatly impressed the friends of national education. A few months before his death, his *Special Report on Elementary Education on the Continent* was reprinted, not by Arnold himself, but with his willing permission. The year following brought the publication of his collected *Reports on Elementary Schools* (1889), under the editorship of Sir Francis Sandford. This work was a compilation of Arnold's annual or biennial reports to the Committee of Council, the authority under which he served. To a student of British education it is an important and interesting book.

There has been, then, a considerable body of Arnold's official discourse to invite attention. A full examination of this reveals, moreover, an affinity between the educational works and the more familiar literary essays. The relationship is particularly close between the official reports and *Culture and Anarchy*, Arnold's most ambitious essay on British social degeneracy and his proposed cultural reform. For in this essay he looked sharply at contemporary things and dealt realistically with their causes and effects. He looked, in fact, at the mid–nineteenth-century stream of social and political affairs with their accompaniment of parliamentary action and inaction. This he viewed from the vantage point of his daily work within the schools and the Education Office; he spoke, in fact, as one informed by his own official observations. There is, then, a continuity of purpose which links the literary side with the official side of Arnold's work. To clarify this common purpose is the object of this study.

In a study of Arnold, it is the strong democratic current of the nineteenth century which gives the proper focus. And likewise, one who reads the history of British education from the context of the present time will perceive a special significance in the great popular movement of that century. Within this interval of a hundred years, the mass of English society was wondrously transformed. At the beginning occurred the founding of two societies dedicated to the education of the poor: the British and Foreign School Society, for the service of Dissenters, and the National Society for Promoting the Education of the Poor in the Principles of the Established Church. Then, an immense impetus to the cause of popular education came with the passage of the Reform acts of 1832 and of 1867. The first grant of state aid for supporting the instruction of the poor was authorized by the House of Commons in 1833; and the establishment of the Queen's Committee of the Privy Council, to supervise the distribution of the grants, occurred in 1839. In 1870 the first comprehensive Education Act was passed by the British Parliament, making the provision of elementary schools mandatory throughout England and Wales. By the Act of 1870, compulsory education was left to the discretion of the newly instituted local school boards; true compulsory attendance was established only through the supplementary Sandor Act of 1876 and the Mundella Act of 1880.

The accompanying social advance, of course, was fraught with bitter conflict between the forces of progress and those of reaction, a conflict in which governments rose and fell. But in the light of its ultimate triumph, it stands as a fascinating pageant of human endeavour. And here for us is the essential point: the principal features of this triumph coincide almost perfectly with the reforms that Matthew Arnold strove to promote throughout his vigorous career as a commentator, as an educator, and as a servant of the state.

It would be difficult to exaggerate the importance of the two school societies in promoting the education of the children of the poor. The first, the British and Foreign School Society, was instituted for the service of religious Dissenters on 22 January 1808 under the leadership of Joseph Lancaster. The second, the National Society, commonly associated with the work of Dr. Andrew Bell, was, as its name implies, devoted to the service of the Established Church. It was formed in October 1811 and incorporated by Royal Charter six years later. Both societies sought to exploit a new monitorial method of teaching, believed to make possible, through a relay of instruction from master to monitors, then from monitors to classes, the education of vast numbers of children, at the cost of only the master's salary and the means necessary for building schools. The method was probably introduced by Dr. Bell, but the impetus for its great popularity certainly came from Joseph Lancaster. Few at that time were able to detect the fallacy of the assumption on which the plan was based, namely, that knowledge could be dispensed and transferred in this mechanical way. Few, however, could envision an education for the poor exceeding the basic skills of reading, writing, and ciphering sufficient for the simple transactions of daily life. The system loomed, therefore, as a bright promise. The prospect was sufficient in itself to arouse an immense national interest in schools.

The vigour of the two new societies should remind us that early popular education was a parochial movement. The fact which must be clearly understood is that the educational enterprise was built upon this foundation of religious purpose. The two societies not only gave the initial incentive to the movement, but they determined in large measure what the character of the schools should be. Because they were charitable institutions, they established an almost insuperable precedent of tenuous support. Also, because they were dedicated to religious instruction, their sponsors were sooner or later prompted to maintain a strong tendency to resist the intervention of the state, the only means by which the education of the poor might attain a tolerable sufficiency.

When the first state grants for education were instituted in 1833, the funds were issued on a matching basis for the two societies to expend. The providing of the grants came about in this way. In the closing days of the parliamentary session (16 August 1833), Lord Althorp, Chancellor of the Exchequer, arose in the House of Commons to offer a "new" resolution, one that required explanation. He was aware, he said, that money advanced by the Government for purposes of education was likely to prove mischievous. He believed that private subscriptions were to be preferred to public money, "but in setting new schools on foot – especially in building school-houses – subscriptions were frequently deficient, and it was for the purpose of building new school-houses that he would now propose that a sum of 20,000 *l.* be granted." The sum, to be placed at the disposal of the Treasury, should be expended only "at the suggestion of the two great School Societies of the kingdom – namely, the National School Society and the Lancasterian School Society."[2]

2 Hansard, *Parliamentary Debates*, Third Series, xx, 730. By the Lancasterian School Society, Lord Althorp meant, of course, the British and Foreign School Society.

Only two members objected to Lord Althorp's motion: Sir Robert Inglis "had never heard an Estimate brought forward in that House with greater surprise than the present. It was the commencement of a new system, the extent of which they could not know. He could not but express his surprise, that such a proposition should have been brought forward without notice, at the very end of the Session, and at two o'clock in the morning." Joseph Hume thought "the plan of giving assistance to schools bad, and there would be no end to the demands for assistance from all parts of the country." He suggested the propriety of postponing action on the resolution "till some plan was formed which would extend to the community in general, or, at all events, till some inquiry could be made as to the propriety of the grant." But without further discussion the motion was agreed to.[3]

The resolution having been carried, the House proceeded on the next day to debate the matter, but with surprisingly little zest. Hume protested that "this miserable pittance would only dry up the sources of private bounty – it would paralyze and prevent the good done by individuals."[4] William Cobbett called the whole subject of education into question:

The Reports that were from time to time laid on the Table of that House, said that men became more and more immoral every year: those Reports must be taken to be true. Then what became of the benefits of education? for education had been more and more spread, but what did it all tend to? Nothing but to increase the number of schoolmasters and schoolmistresses – that new race of idlers. Crime, too, went on increasing. If so, what reason was there to tax the people for the increase of education? It was nothing but an attempt to force education – it was a French – it was a Doctrinaire – plan, and he should always be opposed to it.[5]

The item carried, however, by a vote of 50 to 26. It was indeed "the commencement of a new system." Probably few of the members present could foresee how the assignment of funds would be inevitably followed by inspection, and inspection by control. This innocuous measure, proposed at two o'clock in the morning of one of the strenuous closing days

3 *Ibid.*, 730–1.
4 *Ibid.*, 733.
5 *Ibid.*, 735.

of the session, marks the beginning of the British national system of education.[6]

The clear intent of Parliament was that the grants should be issued only for the building of schools. The sum itself was meagre, but by the end of 1833, sixty-two schools had been aided at a cost to the state of £8,280 14s., and a total cost of £19,380.[7] The manner of payment was established by a Treasury Minute of 30 August 1833, which required that the full amount of the grants be matched by private contributions, expended and accounted for before an application could be considered.[8] This requirement proved to be advantageous to the National Society, which enjoyed an opulent clientele, but it was a considerable hardship to the British and Foreign School Society. The disparity was evident immediately, for, of the sixty-two schools aided by the end of 1833, forty-four were those of the National Society and only eighteen were schools for Dissenters.[9] After five years, the British and Foreign schools had received £30,000 in grants, as against £70,000 given to those of the National Society.[10] The plan also operated with another serious disadvantage: communities with superior resources might augment, by means of the grants, their already ample funds, but impoverished localities must remain destitute through inability to match the government grants; hence, there was no possibility of providing schools where they were most needed.

This informal manner of dispensing government grants continued for six years, but on 12 February 1839, Lord John Russell, a member of Lord Melbourne's Government, appeared on the floor of the Commons, and, "by Her Majesty's command, proposed that the President of the Council and other Privy Councillors, being not more than five persons, should form a board, who should consider in what manner the grants of money made by that House from time to time should be distributed." He notified the House that if the customary grant of £20,000 were made, he should "conduct the measures necessary to carry the objects proposed by the Government into effect." He should prefer, however, an additional grant of £10,000 for establishing a

6 Sir James Edward G. de Montmorency, *The Progress of Education in England* (London, 1904), p. 74 ff.

7 *Ibid.*, p. 76.

8 *Ibid.*, p. 75. The proportion of the local contribution evidently varied according to special circumstances. By 1846 the government was providing about one-third of the total amount.

9 *Ibid.*, p. 76.

10 Henry Bryan Binns, *A Century of Education* (London, 1908), pp. 123-4.

normal school, "for whatever might be the religious differences of the Church and the British and Foreign School Society, yet there must be questions which were not at all touched by their differences ... and he thought it would also be found that there were modes of education, some of which were in operation in foreign establishments, and others in this kingdom, by which the general system of education in this country would be much improved."[11]

Here at last was an overt attack upon the province of the Church, and the tumult was loud and immediate. The Government persisted, however, and on 10 April 1839 issued an Order in Council, appointing a Committee of Council "to superintend the application of any sums voted by Parliament for the purpose of promoting public education."[12]

Still, Parliament failed to recognize a *fait accompli*. On 4 June 1839, Lord Ashley moved a call of the House of Commons for 14 June. The motion was seconded by Lord John Russell and agreed to by the House.[13] The debate lasted for three days, but at the end the committee was upheld by a majority of five votes, with 555 members voting (ayes, 280; noes, 275).[14]

But there lay before the Government still another ordeal: the Commons had yet to move the appropriation of the sums asked for. At the conclusion of a long and turbulent debate, the House divided on the item of £30,000 to be applied to the purposes of education by the Committee of Council, with 275 ayes and 273 noes, that is, by the slender majority of two votes.[15]

The vicissitudes of the Government were, however, but slightly abated. They had yet to bear the violent censure of the Lords, who most stubbornly defended the conservative issues. On 5 July 1839, the Archbishop of Canterbury rose in the Upper House to move a series of six resolutions protesting the action of the Government. The concluding resolution read as follows:

That, under these circumstances, this House considers itself bound by the obligations of public duty to present an humble address to her Majesty, conveying to her Majesty the resolutions into which it has entered, and humbly praying, that her Majesty will be graciously pleased

11 Hansard, Third Series, xlv, 281.
12 Montmorency, p. 84.
13 Hansard, Third Series, xlvii, 1377–8, 1395.
14 *Ibid.*, xlviii, 681.
15 *Ibid.*, 793.

to give directions that no steps shall be taken with respect to the establishment or foundation of any plan for the general education of the people of this country without giving to this House, as one branch of the Legislature, an opportunity of fully considering a measure of such deep importance to the highest interests of the community.[16]

At the conclusion of the debate, the Lords approved the action by a majority of 111 (contents, 229; non-contents, 118), and the resolutions were ordered to be presented to Her Majesty by the whole House.[17]

The address was carried by the peers in procession to Buckingham Palace on Thursday, 11 July. But they had yet to discover the character of their young queen. Her rebuke was firm and unequivocal. She expressed her deep regret that the Lords "should have thought it necessary to take such a step on the Present Occasion." It had been from a deep sense of duty that she had "thought it right to appoint a Committee of my Privy Council to superintend the distribution of the grants voted by the House of Commons for public education." She promised that annual reports should be laid before Parliament, and expressed her full confidence that the funds would be "strictly applied to the Objects for which they were granted."[18] Immediately, the tumult ceased. Both Houses of Parliament accepted the Committee of Council on Education as an established arm of government. And thus was created the authority under which Matthew Arnold was later to serve for thirty-five years.

The item of £10,000 proposed by Lord John Russell for establishing a normal school suggests another important aspect of popular education which developed from the old monitorial system of Lancaster and Bell, the institution of teacher-training. Training schools had been maintained by the two societies in order to supply their own needs. But with the rapid increase of elementary schools under the stimulus of government support, the supply had become more and more inadequate. The new Committee of Council recognized this pressing need and proposed a radical solution. Accordingly, in April 1847, the new Whig Ministry of Lord John Russell, who had succeeded Sir Robert Peel, introduced into both Houses of Parliament some Minutes designed to regulate the apprenticing of pupil teachers. The plan came before the Commons merely as an item of supply, the Committee of Council requesting a grant of £100,000 for this purpose. The item was approved in the

16 *Ibid.*, 1253–5.   17 *Ibid.*, 1332–6.   18 *Ibid.*, XLIX, 128.

Lower House by a large majority despite the strenuous objections of the Voluntaryists, who now opposed all forms of state support as likely to increase the power of the Establishment.

These Minutes, which came to be known as the Minutes of 1846, were designed to improve the method of selecting and training teachers. The basic instruction of the candidates was now to begin in the elementary school itself, while the future teachers were still pupils. The most proficient and promising of the child-monitors were to be selected for apprenticeships lasting from age thirteen to age eighteen. The selections were to be made for the most part from among the children of labourers, whose ordinary prospect had been to leave school at an early age and to begin work for the sake of the few shillings they could add to the family income. But it was in this detail of family income that the good fortune of the selectees was to be immediately realized; for, under the provisions of the new Minutes, the pupil-teachers were to receive stipends, increasing from £10 at the close of the first year to £20 at the close of the fifth, sums far exceeding their probable earnings at the common labour of factory or farm.

Each year these apprentices were to be examined by Her Majesty's inspector in the subjects listed in the regulations. At the end of his apprenticeship, if for any reason he should then decide not to continue as a schoolmaster, every pupil-teacher who had passed the annual examinations would be given a certificate of completion, entitling him to candidacy to one or another occupation under government patronage. Those who chose to continue in their professional course, however, might take an examination, given annually in each inspector's district, in competition for exhibitions as Queen's scholars at a normal school.

Attendance at the normal schools would be still further subsidized by annual stipends of £20 to £25, to be paid directly to the schools. Then, for each student receiving a certificate of successful progress at the end of the first year, the normal school would also receive a bonus of £20; for the second year, the school would receive £25; and for the third, £30. Thus, the training institutions were to be substantially supported, this being one of the prime objectives of the plan.

There were still other benefits from the Minutes of 1846. At the close of the student's training in the normal school, Her Majesty's inspectors would give an examination to determine which one of three degrees of merit he had attained. Every master who left the school with the first (the lowest) degree of merit would be entitled to an annual grant of

£15 or £20; those achieving the second degree would receive annual grants of £20 or £25; and those attaining the highest degree would receive grants of £25 or £30 per annum. This provision of merit awards, however, would be conditional upon the ability of the trustees and managers of the school to which the master went to supply him with a house and with an additional salary equal to twice the amount of the grant.

Thus, a labourer's child might from the age of thirteen enjoy a fairly lucrative progress through a professional course, preparatory to a career "the lowest rewards of which are, that he shall occupy a comfortable dwelling, rent-free, with a salary of £45 or £60 per annum; and which may, if he completes his course of training, be raised to a minimum stipend of £90 per annum."[19]

There were to be still other benefits for the schoolmaster. He might, according to the quality of his own training, instruct monitors and apprentices of his own. Undertaking this responsibility, he must devote to their instruction at least one hour and a half daily during five days of the week, either before or after the regular school hours, receiving for this extra labour an additional annual stipend of £5 for one pupil-teacher, £9 for two, £12 for three, and £3 for every additional one beyond three. The compensation for training stipendiary monitors would be £2 10s. for one, £4 for two, £6 for three, and £1 10s. for each one beyond three. The number of apprentices in any one school would be limited to one for each twenty-five pupils ordinarily attending.[20] Besides these compensations, superannuation pensions were provided for masters distinguished by long and efficient service, or who because of age or infirmity were compelled to retire. Fifteen years of teaching would be the minimum qualification for a pension, seven years of which must have been spent in schools under government inspection.[21]

As a paper plan, the Minutes of 1846 look remarkably auspicious. Something might be said for a system which would enable future teachers to grow up, like children of the stage, in the practice of their life's vocation. The plan did undoubtedly enhance the professional status of the schoolmaster, and arouse, during the early years of his novitiate, his ambitious hope and zealous endeavour. This was the system that Matthew Arnold knew and cherished during the first eleven years

19 Sir James Kay-Shuttleworth, *Four Periods of Public Education* (London, 1862), pp. 480–5.
20 *Ibid.*, p. 537.
21 *Ibid.*, p. 487.

of his inspectorship, the system whose mutilation he was to deprecate when the measure of 1862, known as "Payment by Results," was proposed in Parliament by the leaders of the rising middle class.

And this, in general, was the structure of popular education in 1851, when Arnold became an inspector of schools. There is an interesting anomaly in the manner in which it had been achieved, for, with the exception of voting funds for schools, the legislation of the period had been entirely negative. In the midst of the rival factions, the friends of elementary education had encountered a whole series of defeats in the British Parliament. The Parochial Schools Bill of 1807, Henry Brougham's Bill for the Appointment of a Commission to Inquire into the Abuses of Charities of 1818, Brougham's Education Bill of 1820, Sir James Graham's Factory Bill of 1843 – were all lost amid the animosities of bitter dispute. Not until 1870 would a comprehensive bill for the support of a national system of education succeed in the British Parliament. Meanwhile another method of achieving action had emerged, the issuance of occasional Minutes by the Committee of Council. These Minutes were, in fact, simple executive orders; they depended upon legislative sanction only to the extent of approving the necessary funds. While Parliament argued, therefore, the Committee of Council managed an orderly improvement of the educational resources.

Outside his own Department, Arnold would discover "nothing but jealous classes, checks, and a deadlock." The religious factions had grown more and more adamant as the legislative impasse had deepened. Voluntaryism had become a formidable movement. In the early years of the struggle, the Dissenting groups had strongly favoured government support, only to encounter a mounting tendency, on the parts of both the parliamentary leaders and the later Committee of Council, to placate the Establishment as the only visible means of achieving progress. Even Henry Brougham, who had stood as an old friend and patron of the British and Foreign School Society and had served as one of its vice-presidents – even Henry Brougham had, in a spirit of compromise, included in his Education Bill of 1820 these impossible provisions: that the schoolmaster must be a member of the Established Church, that his qualifications must be certified by the local clergyman, that he must be elected at an assembly of the Church, and that over his election the parson might exercise "not a nominal, but a real and effectual *veto*," that the bishop of the diocese, or the archdeacon, or the dean, or the chancellor might visit the school at any time, and at his own discretion – not acting as a court – might remove the master. These provisions alone, if incorporated into law, would have permitted the dismissal of any teacher trained and employed in the British and Foreign schools.[22]

The Church party had been soundly beaten on the issue of creating the Committee of Council, and yet the defeat had been immediately transformed into a victory. For, on the issue of inspection, the Committee had completely mollified the Churchmen by yielding on the point of official prerogative. Through an arrangement known as the Concordat with the Church, it had agreed that all appointments to inspectorships for Church of England schools should be submitted for approval to the Archbishops of Canterbury and York, who were at liberty also to suggest candidates of their own. The Archbishops were to frame the regulations respecting religious instruction, and the inspectors were required to report to them concerning the methods of inculcating the doctrines of the Church.[23]

The intractability which Henry Brougham had taught the Dissenters in 1820, they were now to relearn under the Committee of Council. Their reactions to the Committee's willingness to conciliate the Church were violent and obdurate. In 1843, therefore, when Sir James Graham introduced his Factory Bill in Parliament, they were ready, in their determination to obstruct any further concessions to their enemies, to betray their own advantages. When Matthew Arnold came to wrestle with the chaotic problems of national education, the constructive partisanship of Dissent had long since been alienated and offended. It would be well to recall these facts later when his displeasure over the stubborn vagaries of Dissent is discovered.

It was a turbulent world that he entered, and one must reflect on its differences from the one that he had known. His own educational opportunities had been about the best that England had to offer – a progress through the public schools and Oxford. He had shared a cultured home, travelled abroad, and enjoyed enlightened companionship. For four years he had known the rich and elegant sophistication of Lansdowne House in London, where he served as the Marquis' private secretary.

22 Hansard, *Parliamentary Debates*, New Series, Commencing with the Accession of George IV, vol. II, 72–6.

23 Francis Adams, *History of the Elementary School Contest in England* (London, 1882), pp. 114–15. Adams states specifically that "the Government refused ... to give the British and Foreign School Society any similar control over the appointment of Inspectors to that enjoyed by the Church." The privilege, however, was extended to the latter society on 12 December 1843 (see Binns, pp. 130–2).

In his own education, Arnold seems to have taken the strangely dedicated and carefree way of genius. As a student at Oxford, he had caused grave anxieties for his family and his serious-minded friends.[24] And yet, we find in the author of the early poems and the prefaces a sustained high seriousness, a quality of mind that is strong and capable. Thus early he had gone far beyond the vestibules of the ancient languages to find delight in the scope and beauty of the classics. His command of the modern European tongues was competent. He revealed a strong sense of historical movements, probably nurtured in part within the family circle by his own historian father. He had the bearing of one who walks daily among the cultured and the well-informed.

Knowing these things, we must reflect – a little apprehensively – that it was a man of this stature who must adapt, now, to the ways of the lower orders. The success with which he did it may be accounted for by the statement of Sir Joshua Fitch: "He whose own thoughts and tastes move habitually on the higher plane is the best qualified to see in true perspective the business of the lower plane, and to recognize the real meaning and value of the humblest detail."[25]

24 Louis Bonnerot has given a fine account of Arnold's student days, with an insight, moreover, into the compelling inner wisdom that caused him to act as he did: "Bien qu'il ait obtenu, la première année de son séjour à Oxford, 'The Hertfordshire Scholarship', en récompense de ses progrès en latin, Arnold, pendant ses années oxoniennes, ne fut jamais enflammé du zèle de Clough et n'accorda aux études qu'un intérêt modéré. Le manque d'application et de sérieux que son père avait noté dès 1840, frappa également William Charles Lake, qui déclare dans ses *Memorials*: 'He showed us both the strong and the weak sides of his character as a scholar, for he was certainly equally brilliant, desultory and idle'. Et loin de s'en cacher ou de s'en corriger, Matthew prenait un plaisir malicieux à se reconnaître tel. Il écrit à J. D. Coleridge en 1843: 'I have been living in perfect quietness – my chief occupation having been abuse of the weather, and my idleness considerable'. Quand les examens approchent, ses amis J. Manley Hawker et Clough surtout, s'alarment. Celui-ci s'impose le rôle de mentor et une activité exemplaire. Mais en vain: Matthew passe une journée entière à la pêche, insensible aux conseils et aux encouragements. Et ce n'est que la veille de son examen qu'il s'occupe d'apprendre à distinguer les philosophes pré-socratiques, chargeant Jowett de lui faire quelques lectures rapides qu'il ponctue d'exclamations comme 'Quels gens remarquables!' Aussi, comme l'avait prévu et prédit Clough, Arnold n'obtint qu'une 'seconde classe' et ce résultat dépassait encore ses mérites. En mars 1845 Matthew Arnold racheta ce demi-échec par l'obtention d'une 'Fellowship' à Oriel, titre que son père avait obtenu juste trente ans auparavant." (*Matthew Arnold, Poète*, Paris, 1947, pp. 27–8)

25 Sir Joshua Fitch, *Thomas and Matthew Arnold and Their Influence on English Education* (New York, 1897), p. 170.

The Origins of *Culture and Anarchy*

I

The Sombre Decade

In 1849 Sir James Kay-Shuttleworth resigned the secretaryship of the Committee of Council on Education and was succeeded by Ralph W. Lingen, Matthew Arnold's former tutor at Balliol College, Oxford. On 21 December 1850, Arnold wrote to his fiancée, Miss Frances Lucy Wightman: "Lingen, who is Education Secretary, and was once my tutor at Oxford, and a genius of good counsel to me ever since, says he means to write me a letter of advice about inspectorships, applying to Lord Lansdowne, etc. Shall I send it on to you?"[1]

Arnold had, since 1847, served as private secretary to Sir Henry Petty-Fitzmaurice, Third Marquis of Lansdowne, President of the Queen's Privy Council, and also president of the Queen's Committee of Council on Education since its institution in 1839. It is not surprising, therefore, that, with two such influential friends to support him, Arnold should have received his offer of appointment as inspector of Her Majesty's schools. The notice came to him on 14 April 1851. To Arnold it was primarily a bread and butter position, providing enough income to permit his marriage, which occurred some two months later on 10 June.

School inspection proved to be a dull and irksome routine, but Arnold applied himself with determined energy and some optimism. On 15 October, he wrote to his wife from the Oldham Road Lancastrian school in Manchester:

I think I shall get interested in the schools after a little time; their

1 *Letters of Matthew Arnold*, ed. George W. E. Russell (London, 1895), I, 13. (Henceforth to be referred to as *Letters*.)

effects on the children are so immense, and their future effects in civilising the next generation of the lower classes, who, as things are going, will have most of the political power of the country in their hands, may be so important. It is really a fine sight in Manchester to see the anxiety felt about them, and the time and money the heads of their cotton-manufacturing population are willing to give to them. In arithmetic, geography, and history the excellence of the schools I have seen is quite wonderful, and almost all the children have an equal amount of information; it is not confined, as in schools of the richer classes, to the one or two cleverest boys.[2]

The account is certainly cheerful, and, even if a little over-sanguine, it foreshadows the studious, contemplative method Arnold would employ in all his professional labours. The constructive character of his work is evident in his first annual report to the Committee of Council in 1852. Here, his concern for the education of the poor pervades his every statement. Already he had discovered that the Wesleyan schools of his Midland district were serving a more fortunate clientele than were the British and Foreign schools,[3] and that hence they were disposed to charge a higher fee in the form of school pence. Arnold looked with disfavour upon these higher fees. He advised that the managers be urged to dispense with the extra charge in order to extend their educational service and "confer on a wider circle the benefits of their excellent schools."[4]

The disadvantages of these higher fees Arnold expounded with plain good sense: "Parents who pay 6d. a week for the instruction of their children are apt to criticize nicely, though not always judiciously, the institution where that instruction is given." They demand privileges for their children, he said, which are likely to embarrass the teacher. They object to having their children serve as monitors, which, for the more

2 *Ibid.*, p. 17.
3 The schools of this society, together with the Wesleyan schools, maintained under a third and separate aegis, were those to be inspected by Matthew Arnold, from his appointment (14 April 1851) until the Education Act of 1870 terminated the denominational system of inspection and provided for a reorganization of inspectorial districts (see *Letters*, II, 53, for Arnold's comment on the change). For a brief statement of Arnold's duties as inspector – the size of his district, and the denominational division of responsibility – see William Bell Guthrie, *Matthew Arnold's Diaries: The Unpublished Items* (Ann Arbor, 1959), I, pp. x–xi.
4 *Reports on Elementary Schools*, ed. Sir Francis Sandford (London, 1889), p. 5.

advanced scholars at least, is itself a valuable experience and one that is essential to the operation of a large school.[5] The teacher's independence deteriorates because his salary must come from the fees which parents pay rather than from remoter sources. Finally, the instruction of the school is disordered by the insistence of the more opulent parents that their children be instructed in proportion to the amount of the fees paid; those who pay most are to be taught most. Consequently, some of the more capable but impecunious scholars are assigned to inferior classes, while incapable ones may be placed in the highest classes despite their inability to learn there.

The insecurity of the master under such circumstances would lead, in Arnold's opinion, to a very serious loss of a salutary discipline. The young inspector was convinced that "there is no class of children so indulged, so generally brought up (at home at least) without discipline, that is, without habits of respect, exact obedience, and self-control, as the children of the lower middle class in this country."[6] At a lower level, he averred, there is a kind of rude discipline derived from adversity, if not from the wisdom of parents; and the upper classes draw from their own enlightenment a disposition to train their children in habits of regular obedience. Where parents are derelict in duty, the responsibility for discipline devolves upon the school; hence, the seriousness of undermining the authority of the teacher, where his hand needs most to be strengthened.

The need for reducing fees to a minimum in the Wesleyan schools applied also, Arnold felt, to those British and Foreign schools which were located in country districts. Here the resources of the Dissenting schools were so inferior to those of the Church of England schools as to make the charging of higher fees practically unavoidable. In the larger towns this was not the case; and here, where resources were fairly ample, Arnold found the best pattern for public education:

here the British schools often have a large and wealthy body of contributors, and here it is that the unsectarian and neutral character of these

5 Arnold's judgment seems right. The monitors would at least receive the first-hand instruction of the master, whereas the other pupils would have to depend upon the relayed, and often diluted or distorted, version of the monitors. For Lancaster's enthusiastic description of the method, see Joseph Lancaster, *Improvements in Education, as It Respects the Industrious Classes* (London, 1805), p. 8.

6 *Reports on Elementary Schools*, pp. 6–7.

schools peculiarly fits them to be common centres, in which the children of a population divided into innumerable sects may be harmoniously educated together. Since, however, this unsectarian character of the British schools often practically operates to their disadvantage in point of support, one is the more anxious that schools based on an admirable principle should at least do nothing to render themselves difficult of access by the establishment of rates of payment higher than those in competing schools in the same locality.[7]

From such a comment one perceives that Arnold quickly discovered the discrimination suffered by the British and Foreign schools in general, and by the rural communities in particular, because of the imperfect system of distributing state grants. He saw also the advantage in the "unsectarian and neutral character" of the Nonconformist schools, a character which "fits them to be common centres" in communities where children of many different religious faiths must be taught together.

There are other significant observations in this first report. In Maesteg, South Wales, Arnold had seen a school maintained without any fees or local contributions other than regular weekly deductions made from the wages of every person employed in the Llynvi Iron Company, the sustaining industry of the town. Married or single, each worker contributed his share; those with large families paid exactly the same amount as those with small ones. Arnold believed that the plan might be made to work elsewhere, if its sponsors were to use a little tact and patience in introducing it.

In weighing such opinions, it is difficult to achieve a reliable perspective – to comprehend, for example, how little was expected at that time from the schools for the poor. Education for the lower orders had, in the popular mind, a status equivalent to other charitable projects. The Sunday schools of the day, surely no more effective as institutions of general education than their counterpart of the present century, were considered an important branch of the total facilities, and were usually included in any official tabulation of educational means. The total cost of a child's education seldom exceeded £1 per year, and this sum was made up of charitable alms, of "school pence" paid by impoverished parents, and of the new government grants amounting to little more

7 *Ibid.*, pp. 10–11. The British and Foreign School Society had, from its institution, provided for: (1) the inclusion of all children desirous of instruction, without regard to church membership or declaration of faith; and (2) the exclusion of all creeds, formularies, or catechisms, both from the instructional and the devotional activities of the school.

than a parsimonious dole. Henry Brougham had complained bitterly in 1839, when the first grant of £30,000 was grudgingly appropriated by the Commons for the latter purpose, that £70,000 – more than twice the amount for education – was voted for building the queen's stables.[8] Many of the proponents of popular education were motivated by a belief that a few tithes expended on rudimentary learning would result in a substantial reduction in the enormous annual outlay for workhouses, prisons, and asylums for the poor. With such ingenuous notions current, even in Parliament, it is not surprising that Arnold, the new inspector, should have expressed a temperate hope. It is possible, too, that he might have shared, at this time, the common attitude of the British educated classes that education for the upper stratum meant one thing, and education for the poor meant quite another.

As for the pupil-teacher system, Arnold was inclined to speak quite favourably of it, but he also saw its imperfections. Already he had uncovered the chief defect in the British methods of education: an exclusive emphasis upon the cramming in of facts. In commenting upon this defect, he revealed his dominant humanistic bent:

But I have been much struck in examining them towards the close of their apprenticeship, when they are generally at least eighteen years old, with the utter disproportion between the great amount of positive information and the low degree of mental culture and intelligence which they exhibit. Young men, whose knowledge of grammar, of the minutest details of geographical and historical facts, and above all of mathematics, is surprising, often cannot paraphrase a plain passage of prose or poetry without totally misapprehending it, or write half a page of composition on any subject without falling into gross blunders of taste and expression. I cannot but think that, with a body of young men so highly instructed, too little attention has hitherto been paid to this side of education; the side through which it chiefly forms the character; ... I am sure that the study of portions of the best English authors, and composition, might with advantage be made a part of their regular course of instruction to a much greater degree than it is at present. Such a training would tend to elevate and humanise a number of young men, who at present, notwithstanding the vast amount of raw information which they have amassed, are wholly uncultivated; and it would have the great social advantage of tending to bring them into intellectual sympathy with the educated of the upper classes.[9]

8 Sir Spencer Walpole, *A History of England* (London, 1886), III, 487.
9 *Reports on Elementary Schools*, pp. 19–20.

Arnold had quickly recognized the futility of cramming facts into uncomprehending heads. The English common schools had developed directly from the monitorial system of Lancaster and Bell. The rote learning of stereotypes was the only method that could be managed by relays of callow child-monitors; even after the monitorial methods had been adapted and improved to become the pupil-teacher system that Arnold knew, the older concept of learning still persisted. Lowndes observed that "there must be thousands of people still alive who can recite the towns of France in alphabetical order: 'Dieppe, Dijon, Dunkirk (querque was too difficult), Havre, Lille, Lyons (pronounced Lions), Marseilles, Montpelier, Orleans, Paris' (pause, then on again)."[10] Ten years after Arnold's first report, Nassau W. Senior, one of the Newcastle Commissioners, was to deprecate the system as still tending to impart mere information rather than to develop the faculties and discipline the mind:

Vast demands are made on the memory, little is done for the improvement of the judgment or reasoning powers. The principle, in short, which the course of study virtually recognises is, to pour into the students' minds a large supply of knowledge which they in turn may discharge into the minds of their scholars, rather than to give them that disciplined intellect which enables a man to obtain for himself and apply information as he wants it. To use a very significant and very intelligible expression, the great feature of the course of study pursued in training colleges is *cram*.[11]

Under this system, Bible history meant learning the names of the kings of Judah and Israel, and the dates of all the minor prophets. Geography meant tracing the wanderings of the Children of Israel, or learning the capitals of the German electorates, or reciting the noteworthy characteristics of Pooree, Benares, Amritsir, Gujerat, Beejapore, and Pondicherry.[12]

But if the schoolmasters thus blindly reinforced the common stereotypes, they had at least one justification to plead, namely, that the inspectorial examinations encouraged just such trivia. One need not return to the nineteenth century to discover the banal influences of central board examinations. The defects of these systems are, of course, height-

10 G. A. N. Lowndes, *The Silent Social Revolution* (London, 1937), p. 13.
11 Nassau W. Senior, *Suggestions on Popular Education* (London, 1861), p. 334.
12 *Ibid.*, p. 340.

ened when, as in Arnold's day, the substance of the test is known to the teachers in advance, for in such cases the instructors see no alternative in promoting their own interests but to rely upon the well-drilled memory of facts.

Considered impartially, Arnold's first report certainly gave evidence of thoughtful insight. After the maturing discipline of experience, the schools would find in him an advocate of abundant power. Already the bases of his more familiar thought were laid: he had reflected upon the perplexing problems of local support and control, of jealous sectarian factions, of dull preoccupation with sterile facts, and of the absence of the edifying humanities. These were the evils against which he would direct his later counsels.

THE YEARS OF RESIGNATION

Ten years were to elapse, however, before Arnold's critical theme would rise above the quiet utilitarian level – ten years, one sadly apprehends, of sombre personal resignation to what must be, of feeling out the mesh, of making truce and giving under. At the end he emerged a man – somewhat less the poet – but a man with eyes aloft upon a new vision. The *Letters* yield the clues to this silent, half-sad metamorphosis – clues that are brief and fleeting, often hidden in the context of intimate report. "This certainly has been one of the most uncomfortable weeks I ever spent," he complained to his wife. "Battersea is so far off, the roads so execrable, and the rain so incessant."[13] And later he wrote from Cambridge: "I have had a long tiring day, and it certainly will be a relief when I get these Eastern Counties over. The worst of it is that invitations to go and see schools are *rained* upon me; and the managers who have held out till now against the Government plan[14] ask me on my father's account to come and inspect them, and to refuse is hard."[15]

His life had become a stultifying race with time and petty appointments.

I got here a little before two [he wrote from Sudbury], had a sandwich,

13 *Letters*, I, 24 (Dec., 1852).
14 Many of the denominational schools had steadfastly refused state grants, choosing to struggle along on their limited resources rather than to repudiate the voluntary principle.
15 *Letters*, I, 24 (Feb. 28, 1853). Arnold's reference to his father here throws an interesting light on the reputation Dr. Thomas Arnold had achieved in his work as headmaster at Rugby (1828–42).

and then went to the school. I don't know why, but I certainly find inspecting peculiarly oppressive just now; but I must tackle to, as it would not do to let this feeling get too strong. All this afternoon I have been haunted by a vision of living with you at Berne, on a diplomatic appointment, and how different that would be from this incessant grind in schools; but I could laugh at myself, too, for the way in which I went on drawing out our life in my mind. After five I took a short walk, got back to dinner at a quarter to six, dined, and started the pupil teachers, and am just writing this to catch the post.[16]

And again, he wrote from Ipswich: "I am too utterly tired out to write. It certainly was nicer when you came with me, though so dreadfully expensive; but it was the only thing that could make this life anything but positive purgatory."[17]

Amid these sombre cares were moments of indulgence. Arnold had still the rich resources of the cultured mind to nourish and sustain him. With his undeviating filial affection, he wrote from Derby:

My Dearest Mother – I have been since Monday at Lincoln, hard worked, but *subsisting* on the Cathedral. Every evening as it grew dark I mounted the hill to it, and remained through the evening service in the nave or transepts, more settled and refreshed than I could have been by anything else. I came down the valley of the Trent to-day. You have no idea what majestic floods! I asked a great deal about them; the new bank at Fledborough[18] has given way, and that place and Ragnall and Dunham are all floating. I astonished the country people by knowing the names of the remote villages by there. I looked affectionately in the bright morning towards Fledborough; my recollections of it are the only approach I have to a memory of a golden age. I thought how I should like once more to see it with you, dearest mother, and to look with you on the gray church, and the immense meadow, and the sparkling Trent. We will talk of it again, for it might be managed from Coleby.[19]

There were late summer holidays at Dover and at Fox How, his mother's home in the Lake Country. "We are going to London by sea tomorrow if it is fine [he wrote to Wyndam Slade from Dover]; it is much cheaper,

16 *Ibid.*, p. 26 (Tuesday, 6 P.M., 1853).

17 *Ibid.*, p. 27 (March 10, 1853).

18 His grandfather, the Rev. John Penrose, was Vicar of Fledborough, Notts.; and his mother was married there in 1820 [Russell's note].

19 *Letters*, I, 23 (Nov. 25, 1852).

and I want to see the Downs, the Nore, Pegwell Bay, etc., which I have
never seen. We go straight on to Fox How on Wednesday or Thursday.
Is it quite impossible for you to come and look at us there in the next six
weeks? It is likely to be fine now, I do really think, even there."[20]

Two months later he was back at work and voicing once more his
nostalgic plaints to his wife:

This must be a scrap, for I must get off as soon as I can in order to get to
Lilleshall, nine miles of cross country road, in time to dress for dinner;
and, while I *am* here, the managers do not like not to be able to talk
to me. I have had a cold, wet journey, and only a bun for luncheon.
I got to Wellington at one o'clock, and came on here – six miles – on
top of an omnibus – a dawdling conveyance, and a cold, wet drive. I felt
rather disconsolate between Liverpool and Shrewsbury ... We have had
such a happy time at Fox How. Then, too, I have had time for employment that I like, and now I am going back to an employment which I
certainly do *not* like, and which leaves me little time for anything else.
I read about fifty pages of *Hypatia*, which is certainly very vigorous and
interesting; however, that did not comfort me much, and I betook
myself to Hesiod, a Greek friend I had with me, with excellent effect;
we will talk about *Hypatia* when we meet.[21]

Now and then his business called him to a university city – to Cambridge
or to his mild mother Oxford. But even here he could not escape the
vexatious miseries of the professional traveller. He wrote to his wife
from Oxford: "I am just back from Whitney; as cold and uncomfortable a life I have had since I left you as one could desire. My bedroom
here is fust and frowsiness itself, and last night I could not get to sleep."[22]

Here amid the familiar scenes of his college days, he was given to
retrospection, for new awarenesses forced themselves upon him; there
were comparisons to be made and judgments to be corrected:

I am writing from Walrond's rooms in Balliol. This time *thirteen* years
ago I was wandering about this quadrangle a freshman, as I see other
freshmen doing now. The time seems prodigious. I do not certainly feel
thirteen years older than when I came up to Oxford ... But I am much
struck with the apathy and *poorness* of the people here, as they now

20 *Ibid.*, p. 37 (Aug. 21, 1854).
21 *Ibid.*, pp. 37–8 (Oct. 17, 1854).
22 *Ibid.*, p. 38 (Oct. 21, 1854).

strike me, and their petty pottering habits compared with the students of Paris, or Germany, or even of London. Animation and interest and the power of work seem so sadly wanting in them. And I think this is so; and the place, in losing Newman and his followers, has lost its religious movement, which after all kept it from stagnating, and has not yet, so far as I see, got anything better. However, we must hope that the coming changes, and perhaps the infusion of Dissenters' sons of that muscular, hard-working, *unblasé* middle class – for it is this, in spite of its abominable disagreeableness – may brace the flaccid sinews of Oxford a little.[23]

The first decade of his inspectorship was a trial by fire for Arnold, a period which stands out clearly, now, as the grand spiritual climacteric of his life. In extremity, he had remembered Goethe's sage resignation: "Homer and Polygnotus daily teach me more and more that our life is a Hell, through which one must struggle as one best can." "I am not very well lately," he told his mother, "have had one or two things to bother me, and more and more have the feeling that I do not do my inspecting work really well and satisfactorily; but I have also lately had a stronger wish than usual not to vacillate and be helpless, but to do my duty, whatever that may be; and out of that wish one may always hope to make something."[24] He had made a deliberate choice; a wife and two sons were now his hostages to fortune; he would do his work with fortitude and resolution.

THE MATURING CRITIC OF BRITISH EDUCATION

Meanwhile Arnold had been multiplying observations and maturing his critical judgment. In 1855, three years after his first report, he was still

23 *Ibid.*, pp. 38–9 (Sunday, Oct., 1854). The laudatory comment on Newman and his followers calls to mind for us the turbulent quarrel of Dr. Thomas Arnold with Newman during the 1830s over church reform (see T. W. Bamford, *Thomas Arnold*, London, 1960, chap. x). The son's comment must reflect urbanity on his part, or at least independence of mind. Louis Bonnerot offers the following opinion: "Plus ondoyant, plus dilettante, Matthew ne partagera jamais l'animosité de son père contre le Catholicisme et le Newmanisme, il ne s'engagera jamais à fond dans aucun débat parce qu'il ne réussira pas à ordonner ses impulsions ni à les diriger vers un but nettement choisi; il s'y efforcera avec persévérance toute sa vie, et ses efforts, constamment renouvelés, le ramèneront insensiblement vers sons père." (*Matthew Arnold, Poète*, Paris, 1947, p. 19)
24 *Letters*, I, p. 41 (Dec. 9, 1854).

perturbed over the failure of the schools to reach the children of the poorest classes; he was harassed, moreover, by popular complaints that the curriculum was too broad, that the standards of scholarship were too extravagant for the cultural needs of the lower strata. Offering anything more than a few rudiments of knowledge on behalf of the poor aroused the resentment of the commercial classes. It is not true, Arnold insisted vehemently,

that the course of instruction in elementary schools generally embraces too many subjects, or is carried on in any of these subjects too far. Certainly it is not true with regard to those elementary schools which I inspect. These are not attended, as I have repeatedly said, by the lowest and poorest classes of children: they are attended often by children who might well lay claim to an instruction of a more comprehensive and advanced kind than that which they obtain in them: they are attended universally by children who may well lay claim, on the score of social position and future prospects in life, to be instructed not only in reading, writing, and the elements of arithmetic, but also in the higher rules of arithmetic – in geography, in English grammar, and in English history.

Arnold comes close here to acknowledging the principle of social stratification, but he hastens to correct any such impression: "I do not mean to affirm it as my opinion, that there are degrees of instruction exactly proportioned to the degrees in society; but I place myself in the point of view of the complainants themselves, and I say, that the children in those schools which I inspect belong to a class for which the complainants themselves would allow that such an instruction as they receive was neither improper nor over-ambitious."[25]

Arnold himself had an eye for the practical and the useful. He was pleased with the introduction of needlework into the girls' schools, and he watched its progress from year to year. In the report for 1858, he was gratified to observe that the girls of the Lancastrian school at Loughborough were bringing work from home, projects begun by their mothers, in need of some judicious correction. The mothers, Arnold observed, were delighted with their daughters' progress; and their earlier superficial interest, limited to fancy and ornamental needlework, had been replaced by genuine respect for plain useful sewing.[26]

His first criticism of the inferior schools of London concerned their

25 *Reports on Elementary Schools*, pp. 53–4.
26 *Ibid.*, p. 80.

lack of supervision by ministers of religion. He cited the special advantage enjoyed by the National schools in the regular pastoral visits of the clergymen, of whose duties the care of the schools was considered a main part. What would have constituted a serious interruption of a layman's daily business, became for the clerical supervisor a customary detail in the planned routine. The managers of the British and Foreign schools, on the other hand, in adhering to the non-sectarian principle, excluded these beneficial pastoral ministrations – in practice if not in principle. The alienation of the clerical arm was still further aggravated in those many cases where congregations elected to unite their schools with the Committee of Council against the pastor's will, an action which often prompted his voluntary withdrawal from all participation in the management of the school.[27]

By the year 1857, Arnold was still more perturbed by the injustice in the method of allotting the government grants – that is, by the principle of granting aid in direct proportion to the munificence of local support. Hitherto he had inspected for the most part schools located in towns (few rural districts were able to qualify for state grants). With the gradual breaking down of denominational antipathy for governmental aid, however, he had been called more and more into the country by managers hopeful of instituting the new system of supplementary support.[28] The result of these visits was for Arnold a new disillusionment. The patrons of these rural schools were poor and few in number. Even though they taxed themselves severely, their means were inadequate for the all-important first step toward qualification for government grants – the securing of a competent well-trained teacher. They invited inspection in the hope of obtaining funds toward the fulfilment of this indispensable first step, only to learn that there was no provision in the Minutes of the Committee of Council that would sanction a preliminary grant. Their reaction to such an apparent injustice was one of bitter disappointment: " 'We have overcome,' they say, 'for the sake of the wants of our ill-provided neighbourhood, the prejudices against state-connection in which we were reared, and after we have made this sacrifice of feeling, and have admitted Government interference, we find the Government refusing to help us, and reserving all its help for those who, far more than we, can help themselves.' "[29]

27 *Ibid.*, p. 44–6.
28 Such visits would represent a supererogatory service on the part of the inspector, whose work was to inspect only those schools actually receiving, or formally applying for, state grants.
29 *Reports on Elementary Schools*, p. 68.

It was inevitable that Arnold must, sooner or later, confront the real limitations of a make-shift structure, and respond by urging the one intelligent corrective. He showed his understanding of the issue in the present instance, and uttered, incidentally, for the first time, what was to become the major tenet in his later essays, namely, the indispensability of a national system of education under the benevolent patronage and control of the state:

They [the rural petitioners] forget, nor would it much console them to remember, that it is in great measure to their own jealousy, to their own past and now confessed prejudices, that their difficulty is attributable. Such an assistance as they demand amounts, in fact, very nearly to the maintenance and support of their school at the expense of the state. The state would contribute the bulk of the funds, and they would contribute the management. The principle of a school system reposing on voluntary local effort is thus abandoned. But what has hitherto made it impossible for the Government in this country to found a national system of education? The loudly-avowed preference for a system of voluntary local effort.[30]

In such a comment one may discern the beginnings of a solid point of view – the assumption of a philosophical position which was to govern all of Arnold's future judgments: his mistrust of the Philistine spirit of independence and its supporting claptrap, his insistence on the national establishment of schools for the rising middle class as the only hope of humanizing their harsh augmenting political control, and his recognition of the ancillary need to develop a truly national system if education were ever to become universal. Here, indeed, the position is expressed by negative implication – by Arnold's protest against the parochial prejudice, against the jealous apprehensions of the Voluntaryists over the benevolent efforts of the state in their behalf. Soon it was to become a strong positive doctrine, underlying the main body of his thought on social and cultural problems – constituting, in fact, the central theme of *Culture and Anarchy* (1869) and a whole group of related essays. Already, in 1857, Arnold had begun to see clearly the one means of relief from the present chaos; the constructive efforts of men in their corporate character, the wise and benevolent action of the state.

Arnold's concern for the national establishment of schools awakened his interest in the administrative and legislative efforts that were being

30 *Ibid.*

made toward this objective. Though his comments on these matters were brief and desultory, they were at least pertinent and practical. In visiting the newly-awakened rural districts, for example, he had noted the lack of competent teachers, a disadvantage resulting from the meagre salaries the rural managers were able to pay. Also, the rapid increase of new schools since the institution of the government grants in 1833 had far outstripped the number of qualified teachers prepared by the normal schools. The Minutes of 1846, it is true, had held out to prospective teachers inducements intended to increase the supply considerably. Among the provisions of these Minutes was an opportunity for the candidate to enter other fields of government service, if, at a later time, he had come to mistrust his aptitude for teaching. But on 12 May 1852 the Committee of Council found it expedient to issue a new Minute, countermanding the option so freely offered and encouraged by the earlier regulation.[31] The Minute of 12 May was undoubtedly intended as a kind of stopgap, designed to prevent the loss of the less successful, but now urgently needed, candidates into other fields of endeavour. Its effect would be to impress more, but less-willing, teachers into the profession in order to ease the extraordinary demand.

Five months earlier, on 10 December 1851, the Committee of Council had issued another Minute of somewhat contrary effect; they had, in fact, established a new step in the training of teachers, that of the assistant-teacher. But the new step, advantageous as it may have been as a training procedure, actually constituted a new hurdle in the pupil-teacher's progress toward the full status of certificated master, namely, an interval of one year spent in residence at a training school under inspection, or a service of three years to be spent as a principal-teacher or as an assistant-teacher in a school subject to inspection. This Minute stipulated further that "after the year 1852, no Candidate (not having been a Pupil-Teacher, or a Student in a Training School under inspection) be admitted to be examined for a Certificate until after he shall have completed his 22nd year, and his School has been inspected and favourably reported upon by one of Her Majesty's Inspectors."[32]

The new requirement must have loomed as a formidable obstacle to those entering the field of teaching. It would, of course, induce many candidates to withdraw into the less exacting fields of government service. The succeeding Minute of 12 May, therefore, was issued to prevent

31 Sir James Kay-Shuttleworth, *Public Education* (London, 1853), p. 131, note.
 See also Hansard, Third Series, LXXXIX, 858–82; and XCI, 952–7.
32 Kay-Shuttleworth, *Public Education*, p. 130, note.

this loss. If new hurdles were to be placed in the way of the candidates in the interests of better preparation, the former alternative of attractive government employment – which was, in fact, only a comfortable means of retreat from the object of first concern – must be withdrawn.

This new concept of assistant-teacher constituted a third step in the hierarchy of apprenticeship: (1) monitor, (2) pupil-teacher, and (3) assistant-teacher. The plan of serving as an assistant under a trained and competent master appears both sensible and practical. Circumstances, however, rendered it almost inoperative. Arnold recognized the causes of the failure and reported them faithfully to his superiors:

But the increase in the number of schools aided by your Lordships, and requiring trained teachers, is at present so rapid, that it still fully keeps pace with, or even outstrips, the supply of such teachers; a student in a training school, therefore, after he has finished the shortest period of training which is permitted, finds no difficulty in at once obtaining his appointment to an elementary school at a principal teacher's salary. There is not at present left, after the existing elementary schools have been provided with principal teachers, any class of students unprovided for, and willing, therefore, to accept a less remunerative, although, for them, more instructive and more improving employment.[33]

For the proper training of the teacher, the times were hardly propitious, and Arnold, accordingly, made concessions to the practical needs of the day. He did not favour any sacrificing of the teacher's status through a voluntary loss of income. Only in a school of the very highest order, offering the most extraordinary advantages as a place of practical training, would he urge the student to accept a position as assistant-teacher with a consequent, though temporary, reduction in salary. Furthermore, the training schools were also faced with the very practical problem of supply. They were responsible first for providing a sufficient number of trained principal teachers for the schools of their own religious denominations. Until these superior positions were filled and a supply of candidates was accumulated beyond this first minimum need, the assistantship as a step in teacher preparation must remain a mere paper plan.

Such were the practical observations which Arnold made during the early years of his inspectorship. Certainly they were pertinent and intelligently conceived. It was in the reflection upon such practical problems that his professional judgment was being formed and expanded.

33 *Reports on Elementary Schools*, p. 71.

Among his comments upon these observations may be distinguished the antecedents of his later thought.

Meanwhile the stream of legislative action had, during these early years of Arnold's service, remained clogged and stagnant. It is a sobering reflection on British legislative history that for the first seventy years of the nineteenth century, a period of intense popular clamour for adequate schools, not one important educational measure received parliamentary approval. The Order of the Queen's Privy Council of 1839, instituting the Committee of Council on Education, together with the several Minutes issued in subsequent years, constituted the only constructive advances in response to an appalling national need. These Minutes were, from the standpoint of democratic procedure, of a questionable character; they were, in fact, neither more nor less than arbitrary executive decrees, forced by the insistence of the Queen's ministers upon the protesting factions in Parliament. Aside from their obvious utility, these Minutes had but one saving grace: they were issued by intelligent and far-seeing statesmen – by men of integrity and good will, whose only fault was a tendency to appease the powerful interests of the Establishment. The representative House of Commons, it is true, had stood officially in a position of practical acquiescence; for not only had it sanctioned the institution of the annual grants in 1833, but it had continued to honour the Council's requests for increased appropriations.

During the first decade of Arnold's inspectorship, there was little variation in the parliamentary deadlock as far as education was concerned. The legislative efforts of the period were, however, marked by a new strategy in that the "comprehensive" system[34] was advocated with rising fervour. Arnold's quick perception of the great advantage of the comprehensive plan, a plan practised consistently in the British and Foreign schools, placed him definitely among the number who favoured this progressive trend. It was now fairly evident to anyone willing to confront obvious facts that the National Society schools, rigidly maintaining their exclusive regulations, could not possibly serve the needs of the heterogeneous population, particularly in those rural districts and

34 The "comprehensive" system was that generally carried on by a religious denomination, providing definite religious instruction of a denominational kind, but allowing parents to decide whether their children should attend or be withdrawn from the religious portion of the programme. The Education Act of 1870 contained a so-called "Time-Table Clause," which required that religious instruction must be given either at the beginning or at the end of the school day, so that the comprehensive easement might be most conveniently observed by the pupils.

small towns where the maintenance of more than one school was obviously impossible. If the schools were to "comprehend" the children of all sects, they must give ground on matters of indoctrination and move toward a secular type of instruction. It was the recognition of this need and the attempt to establish the secular principle that characterize the legislative efforts of the decade. There was also a strong movement toward local government for schools and a growing insistence upon local support by means of "rates" upon taxable property.

These significant trends may be traced directly to a group of interested laymen in Lancashire, who in the autumn of 1847 had formed the Lancashire Public School Association. A year or two later the association was reorganized and renamed The National Public School Association.[35] Under the leadership of Richard Cobden, the new association was dedicated "to promote the establishment, by law, in England and Wales, of a system of Free Schools; which, supported by local rates, and managed by local committees, specially elected for that purpose by the rate-payers, shall impart *secular* instruction only; leaving to parents, guardians, and religious teachers, the inculcation of doctrinal religion, to afford opportunities for which, it is proposed that the schools shall be closed at stated times in each week."[36] From this time forward until the passage of the Education Act of 1870, Manchester became the centre of an agitation for secular, rate-supported schools.[37]

On 26 February 1850, the Hon. William J. Fox, member for Oldham, received permission in the House of Commons to bring in a bill embodying the principles advocated by the National Public School Association. He proposed first "that the deficiency in the supply of the means of education in any parish, or combination of parishes, should be ascertained by Her Majesty's inspectors." With the amount of the deficiency determined, he proposed next "that the locality should be invited to supply it; that the inhabitants of the district should be summoned to elect an education committee, who should have the supply of the deficiency for their peculiar work, and be empowered to rate the inhabitants for the expense necessarily incurred in carrying out their plans." Particular concern for the welfare of existing schools would be maintained; secular education, which should be the special province of the new committees, would be promoted in the existing schools by remunerating the teacher according to the number of pupils who had been efficiently in-

35 To be carefully distinguished from the National Society.
36 "Educational Movements," *Westminster Review*, LIV (January 1851), p. 208.
37 Adams, p. 152.

structed in the elements of secular education, as reported by the inspector. All new schools should be "properly free schools – schools to which any inhabitant of the parish or district should have the right of sending his children, between the ages of seven and thirteen, without charge, without distinction in the treatment and training of the children, with no religious peculiarities inculcated upon them, but with the right reserved and inalienable – the right of the parents to have, at certain convenient times fixed by the master, their children instructed as to religion where and by whom they pleased."[38]

But the friends of the Establishment were quick to recognize in Fox's bill another of the overt attacks for which they had been waiting. The measure was violently opposed as irreligious and atheistic. Sir Henry Howard, the Earl of Arundel and Surrey, exclaimed vehemently against it: "The two armies were drawing up their forces, and the battle was now between religion and irreligion – the Church and infidelity – God and the devil – and the reward for which they must contend was heaven and hell."[39]

It was in vain that the member for Sheffield, the Hon. John Arthur Roebuck, dilated upon the destitution among the poor and the futility of separate and voluntary endeavours to relieve them "when there was a mass of vice beneath them that was absolutely hideous to contemplate." With trenchant scorn he inveighed against Lord Arundel's smug complacency: "Talk to the wretched people, and tell them of the salvation of their souls. Why, it was an impudent mockery."[40]

The bill was doomed from the beginning. It was disposed of by a successful amendment offered by the member for Northamptonshire, the Hon. Augustus S. O. Stafford, which postponed action until a day six months hence (when Parliament would be in recess).[41]

The secular issue, moreover, produced a new pattern of cleavage between the contending factions. Many of the old champions of popular education, including such men as Lord John Russell and Sir James Kay-Shuttleworth, now found themselves within the camp of the opposition. Thus, Lord John, while favouring the introduction of Fox's bill, soon felt called upon to exert his real influence against it because of its secular character and the fact that it offered education gratuitously.

38 Hansard, Third Series, CIX, 38–9.
39 *Ibid.*, CX, 450.
40 *Ibid.*, 454.
41 *Ibid.*, CX, 444–5; and CXI, 792.

And Sir James, the former secretary of the Committee of Council, declared that "no scheme of public education could be more extravagantly rash and arrogant, than one, which would either venture to overlook the religious origin, or the existence and peculiar organization, of so great a number of schools."[42] For the very image of a state school under the democratic management of a local committee not identical with the ecclesiastical vestry, these men entertained a profound and quixotic dread.

Meanwhile, under the guidance of Sir James Kay-Shuttleworth, a rival organization was formed to oppose the efforts of the National Association, namely, the Manchester and Salford Committee on Education. The new organization proposed to raise funds by means of local rates for the support of both secular and religious instruction. The management of the schools and the appointment of teachers were to be given over to the founding denominations. The funds, to be collected by the town councils, were to be turned over to the church authorities, who might act in complete independence of the ratepayers' wishes. The municipalities would be empowered to build any necessary schools, but only after the religious sponsors had failed to exercise their established prerogative to do so. No provision was made in the plan for harmonizing the interests of the rival sects, nor for conciliating their differences. When an attempt was made to impose the Authorized Version of the Bible upon the Roman Catholics, who represented some 100,000 members of the population of the two cities, the latter precipitately withdrew.[43] In the session of 1851, both associations introduced rival bills. That of the National Association was presented by W. J. Fox, and was lost upon the first reading.[44] The other, known as the Manchester and Salford Education Bill, was deferred until the spring of 1852, when, upon its second reading, it appeared that the councils of the respective towns had divided on the merits of the plan. It was eventually referred, together with the bill of the National Public School Association, to a select committee, which sat for two parliamentary sessions, collected a large mass of evidence, and then allowed its efforts to subside without reporting.[45]

On 4 April 1853, Lord John Russell, the President of the Queen's

---

42 Kay-Shuttleworth, *Public Education*, p. 36.
43 Adams, p. 161.
44 *Ibid.*, p. 163.
45 *Ibid.*, pp. 163–4.

Privy Council in the Ministry of Lord Aberdeen, introduced a bill in the Commons known as the Borough Bill, designed to give assistance on the "comprehensive" principle to those schools which, because of local destitution, had hitherto been unable to share in the government grants. With a somewhat devious logic, the Government conceived of the population as divided into two classes, urban and rural. The urban schools were to be the special beneficiaries of the Borough Bill; the rural ones were to be cared for under a convenient Minute of Council. The Borough Bill sought to establish a "capitation" grant of twopence per week per pupil, provided that there were already paid from other sources (charities and school pence) 4d. per week for each girl and 5d. for each boy. The funds for the capitation grants were to be supplied through the assessment of local rates. But the assessment was to be merely optional and permissive; the town councils might, by an affirmative vote of two-thirds of their members, impose a rate for the purpose of improving education. The rate might be applied, "not to establish schools in substitution of former schools, but in aid of the voluntary efforts of individuals, and in aid of the school pence given by the parent."[46] The bill would avoid the touchy religious problem by the inclusion of a convenient clause which allowed a parent "the power of withdrawing his child from the religious instruction to which he might be subjected."[47]

The apathy of the Commons to Lord John Russell's bill was such as to cause the Government to abandon the measure without effort. The executive power of the Committee of Council was, however, now brought into sharp contrast with the ineffectuality of the legislative methods; for the rural districts (agricultural parishes and unincorporated towns with no more than 5,000 inhabitants) received, through the authority of a Minute of Council, a most welcome but unexpected subsidy. The Minute provided a capitation grant of seven shillings per pupil for all boys and five shillings for all girls who attended school on an average of four days per week during forty-eight weeks of the school year, or 192 days. The grant was also contingent upon the payment of at least one penny per week by the parents of each pupil, upon the master's holding a certificate under the provisions of the Minutes of 1846, and upon the successful passing of the examinations of Her Majesty's inspector by at least three-fourths of the pupils between seven and thirteen years of age.[48]

46 Hansard, Third Series, cxxv, 536–7.
47 Ibid., 538.
48 Kay-Shuttleworth, Public Education, pp. 305–7.

As a result of this Minute, the annual grant for education rose immediately from £160,000 to £260,000[49] to the exclusive advantage of the better schools of the rural districts; and when, in January 1856, the benefit was extended to the whole country, the grant rose another £200,000.[50]

The effect of these executive actions was an immense increase in the subsidization of the Establishment, which stood in control of some four-fifths of the schools receiving the benefit. The consistent policy of the Committee of Council was at last apparent to all the leaders of Dissent: it had abandoned the one substantial hope of the nation, the establishment of a true national system of tax-supported schools; in effect, it had chosen to conciliate the vested interests of powerful and influential groups.

Several other bills were offered during the remaining years of the decade, but all of them of any consequence were lost or abandoned amid the tumult of conflicting interests.

To most of this legislative effort Arnold remained silent and aloof. He mentions, in fact, but one measure in the whole body of his personal correspondence for the period. In a letter of 31 March 1856 to his sister "K" (Mrs. William E. Forster) he says briefly: "I see Baines has poured himself out in to-day's *Times*. Lord John's measure is said to be of Shuttleworth's concoction, and if so, I think it will succeed, for Shuttleworth knows better than most people what will go down in the way of education."[51]

The "measure"[52] to which Arnold alludes had not even the status of a pending bill. Lord John Russell had, on 6 March 1856, merely placed before the House of Commons a set of twelve resolutions, a discussion of which, he hoped, might serve to clarify the major issues and to reveal the temper of the members in regard to the preparation of a tentative education bill.[53] Of the twelve resolutions, the first five dealt merely with a consolidation of the Minutes of the Committee of Council and a proposed reorganization of inspectorial districts in terms of better denominational representation. The remaining seven covered the chief issues of the Voluntaryist and Secularist controversies. If embodied into law, the positive principles of these resolutions would provide for: com-

49 Hansard, Third Series, cxxi, 1415; and cxxvii, 417.
50 Adams, p. 167.
51 *Letters*, I, 50–1 (March 31, 1856).
52 Not to be confused with Lord John Russell's Borough Bill of 1853.
53 Hansard, Third Series, cxl, 1955–80.

pulsory local taxation for educational purposes under the power and authority of the magistrates of the quarter sessions (no. 8) ; local control by a school committee, with power to appoint the teacher and manage the school (no. 9) ; compulsory daily reading of the Holy Scriptures, but with a protective conscience clause permitting parents or guardians to withdraw their children from religious observances without penalty (no. 10) ; and compulsory education for all children employed between the ages of nine and fifteen, at the expense of the employer (no. 11).

It was the public discussion of these resolutions that had aroused the apprehensions of Edward Baines, editor of the *Leeds Mercury*, who, with Edward Miall, stood among the staunchest leaders of the Voluntary movement. Baines served under the aegis of the Congregational Board of Education, which had stood rigidly opposed to all forms of government intervention in the management of schools.

The article which had elicited Arnold's comment had appeared in the London *Times* on 31 March 1856, under the heading of "Lord John Russell's Plan of Education."[54] Both the article and Arnold's brief statement regarding it are important, for together they stand as evidence of Arnold's growing revulsion against the Philistine doctrines which so sorely complicated the political, the social, and the industrial issues of his day. It was the florid rationalizations of such men that Arnold was to deprecate in *Culture and Anarchy* under the name of "claptrap." These were the men he castigated as resenting any form of governmental restraint; it was they who gloried in the arrogant right of every Englishman to do invariably whatever he pleased.[55]

Even from the perspectives of the present day, there is a familiar ring to the plain "practicalities" of Edward Baines. He organized his objections to Lord John's resolutions under nine heads. "First of all, the plan is despotic in its character." It *compels* parishes to provide schools, and it *forces* employers to pay for them. "This is an outrage on British freedom." "If it should apparently succeed in bringing a certain number of children under education, it will do it at the expense of that liberty which is more important than education itself." Then there is the patent inability of governments to manage ordinary business affairs. It is universally acknowledged, Baines says, that governments are "the worst of cultivators, the worst of manufacturers, and the worst of traders. ... What hope can there be that they will efficiently manage the infinitely

54 Vol. 329, no. 22, p. 12.
55 See Patrick J. McCarthy, *Matthew Arnold and the Three Classes* (New York, 1964), chap. v.

delicate and important work of education?" The mere undertaking of it would be "another step toward centralization, and toward that bureaucracy which is a poison and a curse to every nation on whom it is imposed."

There is obvious misrepresentation in Baines's assessment of the costs upon the poor. "To the poor," he insists, "it would be a most severe affliction," for their children would be driven from their present lucrative employments. And then, with what looks like callous candour, he quotes the census figures of 1851 on the numbers of children employed industrially in England and Wales. The tabulation begins with five-year-olds, 1,205 of whom are engaged in industrial employment. The figures rise steadily as the age of the children increases to fourteen years, with 203,300 employed at the highest level. The total number of children employed between and including the ages of five and fourteen is approximately 600,000. Baines estimates the income of these children, earning on the average two shillings per week, at £60,000 a week, or £3,120,000 per year; and even if they were to average only a shilling and sixpence a week, he says, they would bring in £45,000 per week, or £2,340,000 a year. "Such is the produce of juvenile labour to the families of the poor; and a large part of this would be taken away by Lord John Russell's plan. In addition to this loss, every father of a family would have to pay a school-rate."

It was the desire of middle-class tradesmen and manufacturers to protect their interests in these practices that inspired the Philistine argument. Their weapon often was deceit; with self-assured plausibility, they completely overlooked obvious evils in threatening greater ones if the sacred rights of Englishmen to do exactly as they pleased were in any way infringed. The use of frightening generalities was their favourite mode of appeal:

Thus, instead of increasing the amount of education in the country, Lord John Russell might by his despotic law actually diminish it. The elder children would in a great many cases not continue at school, but be idle in the streets, exposed to temptation and liable to swell the number of juvenile criminals; while the younger children would also be in the streets, because their parents had lost the help formerly received from the elder. Such would, probably, be the consequence of attempting to force education beyond the point which public opinion warrants. No one would be more desirous than myself to induce parents by moral suasion to lengthen the term of their children's education; but this is a moral work, requiring time and patience; and to attempt to lengthen education by pains and penalties would recoil upon the country with complicated disaster and evil.

Baines follows with the common stereotypes of popular appeal: The cost of the scheme would be enormous, actually more than the whole amount of the poor rates.[56] "A pleasant prospect, truly, for the farmers and other rate-payers! A tolerable 'price' to pay for the 'whistle' of Government education!" And then, of course, the measure is unnecessary, for the noble efforts of the people, the zeal of the religious communities, have been bountifully rewarded. "If these natural motives are not to be trusted, then there is no lesson to be learnt from experience, nor is any faith or confidence due to the great principle of freedom." And finally, there was the awesome apparition of governmental persecution, whereby Dissenters might be compelled to contribute to the propagation of alien faiths, or, worse still, to forego the inculcation of their own doctrines while forced to "comprehend" the children of other creeds within their own schools.

As for Baines's claims concerning the adequacy of the present system, Earl Granville had, during the course of the debate, presented some figures which should have afforded ample disillusionment: "It appears by the Census returns that there are 5,000,000 of young persons in England between the ages of five and fifteen years, 2,000,000 of whom it was stated attended schools, receiving more or less education therein; 1,000,000 were kept almost constantly at work; while there were 2,000,000 who were neither employed nor received any education whatever."[57]

Baines's stand on this issue presents an interesting problem in social perspective. As a leading liberal, he had fought for the repeal of the corn laws, and had strongly supported Catholic emancipation. It was Edward Baines who, in 1830, had proposed the candidacy of Henry Peter Brougham as member for Yorkshire. A life-long Sunday-school teacher and advocate of total abstinence, he appears to have been a

56 Lord John Russell had estimated the total cost of his plan at about £3,240,-000 a year, this amount to be raised "partly by subscriptions, partly by school pence, partly by grants, partly by charitable endowments, and partly by rates" (Hansard, Third Series, cxl, 1980). Baines set his estimate at £6,000,000 or even £7,000,000 a year, all of which, he alleged, must be raised by rates and taxes.

57 Hansard, Third Series, cxli, 37.

sincerely religious man, devoted to social progress and good works. But as a leader of the Voluntaryist movement, he was adamant in his stand against any governmental intrusion upon the educational prerogatives of the denominations. When such idealistic motives became entangled with the aims of free trade and industrial *laissez-faire*, they produced a strange amalgam, as his apology for child labour clearly shows.[58] His arguments represent fairly the motives and the methods of the Voluntaryists. Against the schemes of such special pleaders, there could be but one effectual remedy, the one that Arnold began to advocate in his second annual report (1853): the perfection of the very instrument which Baines and his Philistine faction sought to suppress, that is, universal education for the poor under state control. This means lay beyond the reach and the desire of the masses, who, in their extremity, had resorted to the exploitation of their own children. The means of their relief must, as Arnold now saw clearly, be mandatory: "and I am far from imagining that a lower school fee, or even a free admission, would induce the poor universally to send their children to school. It is not the high payments alone which deter them; all I say is, as to the general question of the education of the masses, that they [fees] deter them in many cases. But it is my firm conviction, that education will never, any more than vaccination, become universal in this country, until it is made compulsory."[59] Arnold had learned this lesson in the very first years of his novitiate; he had discovered the disingenuous motives of the Philistine opposition, and he had upheld the instrument which they most hated and feared, compulsory attendance in schools provided and controlled by the state.

Lord John Russell's resolutions, although they formed the subject of a heated debate, came in the end to nothing. Depending as they did upon an enabling act, they received no such support from the hesitant leadership of Lord Granville, the President of the Council under the Palmerston Ministry. During the course of the debate, Lord John found it expedient to withdraw the most important of his resolutions, retaining only the first five, those pertaining to the reorganization of the inspec-

---

58 Baines, in 1935, published a *History of the Cotton Manufacture of Great Britain*, "still a standard authority" (*Dictionary of National Biography*, Supplement, vol. 1). He served in Parliament as member for Leeds from 1859 to 1874. Upon his defeat in the latter year, he received a letter from Gladstone commending his "single-minded devotion, courage of purpose, perfect integrity, and ability." In November 1880, he received the accolade of knighthood.
59 *Reports on Elementary Schools*, pp. 26–7.

torial service. Even this compromise was unavailing; he was effectually dispossessed of the floor, and his "measure" was lost.

THE NEWCASTLE COMMISSION

It was now fully apparent that no constructive education measure could be looked for with Parliament in its present temper. Throughout the country there was deep unrest over the failure to relieve the educational destitution, but the factional deadlock held. In February 1858, however, the efforts of the friends of education received a new impetus and took a new direction. Lord Derby's Ministry went into office that month, with Sir John Pakington, one of the strongest supporters of Lord John Russell's resolutions and the several secular bills, as one of its members. On the eleventh day of the month, this able leader made a motion on the floor of the Commons: " 'That an humble Address be presented to Her Majesty, praying that She will be graciously pleased to issue a Commission to inquire into the present state of popular Education in England, and whether the present system is, or is not, sufficient for its object; and to consider and report what changes, if any, are required for the extension of sound and cheap Elementary Instruction to all classes of the People.' "[60]

Despite a scurry of alarm on the part of the obstructionists, the motion carried by a majority of sixty-one votes. Four days later the Queen's answer was reported to the House: " 'And having taken the subject into consideration, I have directed that a Commission shall issue for the purposes which you have requested.' "[61] Thus was created what came to be known as The Duke of Newcastle's Commission, after the name of its able chairman.

The appointment of the Newcastle Commission marked the end of a dull and melancholy period in Arnold's life, and the beginning of one that was brilliant with creative power. On 25 January 1859 he wrote to his sister "K":

The night before I got your letter I heard from Stephen, the Secretary of the Education Commission, asking me to call upon him, and I saw him yesterday. He proposed to me to go as the Foreign Assistant Commissioner of the Commission to France and the French-speaking countries – Belgium, Switzerland, and Piedmont – to report on the systems

60 Hansard, Third Series, CXLVIII, 1198-9, 1248.
61 Ibid., 1372.

of elementary education there. There are to be two Foreign A. cs.,[62]
one for France, one for Germany. I cannot tell you how much I like the
errand, and above all, to have the French district.[63]

Amid the querulous thinking that had marked the debates on the educational issues in Parliament there had been scattered allusions to foreign
systems of such reputed merit as should have moved the self-satisfied
Englishman to shame. Most of these references were of an obscure, an
apocryphal, sort. One of the wise decisions of the Newcastle commissioners was to dispatch assistant commissioners to the Continent, instructing them specifically "to obtain from the countries to which you may be
sent as broad a view as possible of their general systems of education, the
manner and degree in which they are practically carried out, and their
effects on the population."[64]

Arnold's appointment to this important mission came to him as a
great release. On 16 February 1859, he wrote again to Mrs. Forster:

I thought of starting next Monday week, but I shall hardly be ready by
that time, besides, I think of being presented at the *levée* on 2nd March,
in order to be capable of going to Courts abroad, if necessary. I like
the thoughts of the Mission more and more. You know that I have no
special interest in the subject of public education, but a mission like
this appeals even to the general interest which every educated man cannot help feeling in such a subject. I shall for five months get free from
the routine work of it, of which I sometimes get very sick, and be
dealing with its history and principles. Then foreign life is still to me
perfectly delightful, and *liberating* in the highest degree, although I get
more and more satisfied to live generally in England, and convinced
that I shall work best in the long-run by living in the country which is
my own. But when I think of the borders of the Lake of Geneva in
May, and the narcissuses, and the lilies, I can hardly sit still.[65]

62 Arnold and the Rev. Mark Pattison.
63 *Letters*, I, 77. Super gives the date of Fitzjames Stephen's letter of notification
   to Arnold as 25 January 1859 (*The Complete Prose Works of Matthew
   Arnold*, ed. Robert H. Super, Ann Arbor, 1962, II, 328, hereafter cited as
   Super). If this is true, then Russell's dating of Arnold's letter to "K" is obviously wrong, as Super's note states.
64 *Reports of the Assistant Commissioners Appointed to Inquire into the State
   of Popular Education in England* (London, 1861), IV, 7.
65 *Letters*, I, 78-9.

II

The Young Liberal in France

Emerging thus fortuitously from his discontent, Arnold plunged into amazing action. The circumstances of his transformation are somewhat anomalous; there had been so little in his recent utterance to suggest the new direction. He had been a poet, and, more lately, a faithful reporter on the condition of Her Majesty's schools. Now, after five months on the Continent, he stood forth as a political and social philosopher with insights into the causative power of the popular will. Witnessing this strange awakening, one is immediately curious concerning the indifference Arnold had hitherto displayed toward matters of political and legislative importance. Throughout the sombre fifties he had had so little to say about the chaotic state of current affairs. Before he had returned from France, he had published his illuminating pamphlet, *England and the Italian Question* (August 1859), his first political essay.[1] Instantly, with this new venture, Arnold displayed an impressive power as a commentator on international matters; and one reflects, a little puzzled, that these have not the small dimensions of incipient growth. Where had lain the antecedents of this strange new interest; or, if it had existed heretofore, what had hidden for a time this vigorous propensity?[2]

The best clues are to be found in the letters of 1848, the revolutionary year in Europe. The overthrow of Louis Philippe had brought forth a

---

1 See Merle M. Bevington, *Matthew Arnold's England and the Italian Question* (Durham, 1953), "Introduction," for the story of the publication and the historical events that inspired it.

2 See Super's comment, beginning "The failure of Arnold's pamphlet ... ," on what he considers the shortcomings of Arnold's "amateur diplomacy" (Super, I, 235–6).

long correspondence between Arnold and Arthur Hugh Clough, in which many of the new ideas were articulated – ideas that were to recur often throughout the years of Arnold's maturity and to reach a strong culmination in his *Culture and Anarchy*. There was in these early letters, for example, a brooding certainty of social change – of shifting power among the social levels – which Arnold, though he mistrusted the revolutionary instrument thereof, viewed, nevertheless, with some complacency. On 1 March 1848, he wrote to Clough:

As to my news Lord L[ansdowne] told it me, and it came from a Govt. messenger – who seems however to have shared the cock-and-bull – prolific excitement of common men at these moments. Yesterday I taxed the hoary communicator: and he owned that the assertion was premature: but declared that numbers of Gig-owners were entering the N [ational] G [uard] in that view: and instanced the duc de Guiche. However I think Gig-owning has received a severe, tho: please God, momentary blow: also, Gig-owning keeps better than it re-begins. Certainly the present spectacle in France is a fine one: mostly so indeed to the historical swift-kindling man, who is not over-haunted by the pale thought, that, after all man's shifting of posture, restat vivere. Even to such a man revolutions and bodily illnesses are fine anodynes when he is agent or patient therein: but when he is a spectator only, their kind effect is transitory.[3]

From Lansdowne House in London, he writes less cryptically to his sister "K":

It is so hard to sequester oneself here from the rush of public changes and talk, and yet so unprofitable to attend to it. I was myself tempted to attempt some political writing the other day, but in the watches of the night I seemed to feel that in that direction I had some enthusiasm of the head perhaps, but no profound stirring. So I desisted, and have only poured forth a little to Clough, we two agreeing like two lambs in a world of wolves. I think you would have liked to see the correspondence.

What agitates me is this, if the new state of things succeeds in France, social changes are *inevitable* here and elsewhere, for no one looks on seeing his neighbour mending without asking himself if he cannot mend in the same way; but, without waiting for the result, the spectacle of France is likely to breed great agitation here, and such is

3 Howard Foster Lowry, *The Letters of Matthew Arnold to Arthur Hugh Clough* (London and New York, 1932), p. 68 ff.

the state of our masses that their movements now *can* only be brutal plundering and destroying. And if they wait, there is no one, as far as one sees, to train them to conquer, by their attitude and superior conviction; the deep ignorance of the middle and upper classes, and their feebleness of vision becoming, if possible, daily more apparent. You must by this time begin to see what people mean by placing France *politically* in the van of Europe; it is the *intelligence* of their *idea-moved masses* which makes them, politically, as far superior to the *insensible masses* of England as to the Russian serfs, and at the same time they do not threaten the educated world with the intolerable *laideur* of the well-fed American masses, so deeply anti-pathetic to continental Europe.[4]

The "please God, momentary blow," said of the genus Gig-owner,[5] reflects Arnold's temperamental conservatism. In the expression of his liberal views, he never overlooks, amid his hopes for change, an immense cultural heritage – an accretion not to be despoiled by insensate hordes. This position he shared with Burke, whose disciple and editor he became.[6] "Gig-owning keeps better than it re-begins." Here Arnold's meaning is that while this feudal relict must be superseded, there is much in its lineage that must be salvaged. Its mellow tradition of gentility and generous living must be distilled and diffused rather than delivered over to the obtuse mercies of the mob.

Also to be especially noted in these early letters is Arnold's affinity for the French. Against the coarse bestiality of the English masses, he juxtaposed the sensitivity and finesse of the Gaul. Among the "idea-moved masses" of France, the revolution might prosper; but its agitation, when borne across the channel to the "insensible masses of England," would lead to brutal plunder and destruction. And herein, even at this early date, lies an educational implication; for with poignant regret Arnold reflects that there is no one to train these British masses to rule, "the deep ignorance of the middle and upper classes, and their feebleness of vision becoming, if possible, daily more apparent." It is France, her Goddess of Lubricity not yet exalted, that stands politically in the van of Europe.

Arnold's admiration for the French was no light or transient fancy. Eighteen years later, in *Friendship's Garland* (1866), he speaks through

---

4 *Letters*, I, 5–6 (Friday, March 10, 1848).

5 Carlyle had used the term as symbolic of the aristocrats.

6 Edmund Burke, *Letters, Speeches, and Tracts on Irish Affairs*, coll. and arr. Matthew Arnold (London, 1881).

the mouth of Arminius, Baron von Thunder-ten-Tronckh, his wise but cynical *alter ego*:

The French are not solid enough for my taste; but, *Gott in Himmel*! that people has had a fire baptism, and the democracy which is born of a fire baptism like theirs, "Geist" [intelligence] cannot help caring about. They were unripe for the task they in '89 set themselves to do; and yet, by the strength of "Geist" and their faith in "Geist," this "mere viper brood of canting egotists" did so much that they left their traces in half the beneficial reforms through Europe; and if you ask how, at Naples, a convent became a school, or in Ticino an intolerable oligarchy ceased to govern, or in Prussia Stein was able to carry his land-reforms, you get one answer: *the French*! Till modern society is finally formed, French democracy will still be a power in Europe, ...[7]

The letters to Clough give us other leads into the veiled region of Arnold's early social and political thought. He had, for example, by his twenty-sixth year, peered deeply into the troubled waters of industrial unrest, and perceived a philosophic truth far below the surface of the capital-labour quarrel:

– Don't you think the eternal relations between labour and capital the Times twaddles so of have small existence for a *whole society* that has resolved no longer to live by bread alone. What are called the *fair profits* of capital which if it does not realize it will leave its seat and go else-where, have surely no absolute amount, but depend on the view the capitalist takes of the matter. If the rule is – everyone must get all he can – the capitalist understands by *fair profits* such as will enable him to live like a colossal Nob: and Lancashire artisans knowing if they will not let him make these, Yorkshire artisans will, tacent and sweat. But an apostolic capitalist willing to live as an artisan among artisans may surely divide profits on a scale undreamed of Capitalisto nobefacturo. And in a country all whose capitalists were apostolic, the confusion a solitary apostle would make, could not exist.

7 Super, v, 45–6. For a good speculation on the early French influences, includ-
ing Arnold's boyhood trips abroad with his father, see Frank J. W. Harding,
Matthew Arnold, the Critic, and France (Genève, 1964). As the title suggests,
the influences appear to be literary rather than political – quite like the
Oxford lectures in temper ("Maurice de Guérin," "Eugénie de Guérin,"
"Joubert," and "The Literary Influence of Academies").

– Answer me that. If there is necessity anywhere, it is in the Corruption of man, as Tom[8] might say, only. –[9]

Surely, here beneath the flippancies of Arnold's manner flash the insights of the liberal mind. Through the deluge of cant poured forth by the Bounderbys of Coketown, Arnold has discerned the power of mankind's collective capability, the higher reaches of human living which, he believes, are indeed to be had in proportion to man's spiritual insistence – in direct ratio to the obduracy of his refusal to live by bread alone.

The letters echo the troubles of the times: the sullen misery of the labouring classes, the failure of the Reform Act to ameliorate their lot, the cruel dialectic of industrial *laissez-faire*, the ominous violence of the new Chartist uprisings, the Paris Revolution with its seismic waves threatening the English dependabilities. They remind us, too, of the preoccupations of the young Oxford intellectuals, especially the stirring discussions they had in each other's rooms. John Duke Coleridge, the future Lord Chief Justice of England, preceded Arnold at Balliol by some two years. He tells us of the "Decade" club, and through the faulty memory of John Campbell Shairp gives us an imperfect list of its members:

Who has the books of the Decade I do not know, and I cannot pretend from memory to give a list of its members. But amongst them, Shairp found when he joined it, Sir Benjamin Brodie (the second Baronet), Deans Church, Lake and Stanley, Bishop Temple [Temple must have been the second undergraduate member, in July 1840], the present Master of Balliol [Jowett], Arthur Clough, Matthew Arnold, James Riddell, John Seymour, I think Lord Lingen [a mistake], Constantine Pritchard, Theodore Walrond, Canon Butler, and a number more whose names have faded from a memory decaying, or perhaps, like the club, decayed. We met in one another's rooms. We discussed all things, human and divine. We thought we stripped things to the very bone, we believed we dragged recondite truths into the light of common day and subjected them to the scrutiny of what we were pleased to call our minds. We fought to the very stumps of our intellects, and I believe that many of us, I can speak for one, would gladly admit that many a fruitful

8 Matthew's younger brother. He and Matthew, Clough, and Theodore Walrond were inseparable companions at Oxford. The four had breakfasted together regularly in Clough's rooms at Oriel on Sunday mornings.

9 Lowry, pp. 68–9.

seed of knowledge, of taste, of cultivation, was sown on those pleasant, if somewhat pugnacious evenings.[10]

The evidence of the letters is, of course, somewhat tenuous. They shadow forth, nevertheless, a semblance of the early context, and give with sure fidelity the temper of Arnold's present thought. And they may explain what the liberating air of France called forth on a later occasion. The anomaly lies in the long cessation of so potent, so vigorous a stream. What the letters most clearly reveal is the philosophic cast of Arnold's intellect; he sought habitually, beyond the facts of observation, to discover the interrelationships of things. His interests therefore fell into connected patterns and suffer loss of significance if dissociated or detached. His educational thought was no exception; about it lay a pattern of historical and contemporary affairs made up of many elements. If he was pessimistic over the decline of British foreign prestige,[11] it was because of the eclipse of the old aristocracy, the professional ruling class. Having "something rare and admirable in itself," its tradition of gentility and good manners was now being violently overborne by the gaucheries of the rising middle class. The glory had departed, and by one means alone was the restoration to be made: by a new diffusion of sweetness and light.

It is only by recognizing this, his essential habit of thought – his method of attacking problems, not singly, but with all their complex relationships fully considered – that Arnold's activities in France can be explained. He had come on an educational mission, but he could not be restrained by such a limitation. He gives us here a demonstration of his critical method: writing first a political pamphlet, then his official report on educational matters abroad, and then finally a philosophical preface by which he wanted his central message to be introduced. He took, moreover, an excursion into the field of secondary education, quite beyond the range of his assignment, and collected the data for his next literary venture, *A French Eton* (1864).

The political pamphlet, *England and the Italian Question* (1859), deals with the intervention of the French under Louis Napoleon, against the Austrians in Italy.[12] It is an exposure – so Arnold intended it to be –

10 Ernest Hartley Coleridge, *Life and Correspondence of John Duke Lord Cole-ridge* (London, 1904), I, 76–7. The brackets represent Lord Coleridge's attempt to correct Shairp's list.
11 *Letters*, I, 39–40 (Ampthill, Wednesday, 1854; Derby, Nov. 6, 1854).
12 Super, I, 65 ff. See especially Super's account of the events that inspired Arnold's pamphlet (pp. 234–6).

of British ineptitude for international politics, and an exposition of the brilliant acumen of the French people, including the Emperor, for such things. The condemnation of the French action by the English aristocracy, Arnold said, was justified; but every reason that it had advanced in support of its judgment was wrong, these reasons being, of course, demonstrable evidences of British obtuseness in foreign affairs. He arraigned the English aristocracy for three false assumptions: one, that the Italian people, having never since the fall of the Empire been independent of foreign rulers, had shown clearly their incapacity for self-determination; two, that the principle of homogeneous nationality under which the Italians claimed their right to independence was for them chimerical; and three, that the intervention of the French was purely a war of conquest, intended to substitute, for the Italians, a French instead of an Austrian domination.[13] Arnold's refutation of the first two "false assumptions" reflects a surprising erudition in historical studies; it is not, however, of much significance here. It is his discussion of the third fallacy that leads to the more important concepts which are to reverberate through his later essays, both those on education and those in the more familiar realm of *belles lettres*.

First of all, Arnold had enough insight into political matters to understand thoroughly, and to confront placidly, the full implications of the ideas which had inspired the French Revolution and of those which emanated therefrom. He sympathized with those ideas and understood their ineradicable effect upon the intellectual cosmos. Politicians, he said, have used and abused these ideas for seventy years, "but no politician has played a great part without taking them into account." With the masses of the people, always strongly susceptible to the powerful tides of popular opinion, these ideas still abide as an irrepressible aspiration, a silent, innate, universal conviction. Hence, the common people respond with enthusiasm when questions of "the abolition of privilege, the right of a people to choose its own government, or the claims of nationalities are involved." They have, on the other hand, "little regard for considerations of policy, of respect for established facts, of compromise. They possess the graver fault of having little regard even for justice, except under a poetical and popular form. At any rate, the considerations above mentioned find them singularly deaf."[14]

Surely Arnold's drift is unmistakable: he looked for the springs of political progress and change, not in the Court or the Senate, but in the oracular mind of the people. "At the present juncture," he said later in

13 *Ibid.*, p. 65.
14 *Ibid.*, pp. 81–2.

Culture and Anarchy, "the centre of movement is not in the House of Commons. It is in the fermenting mind of the nation; and his is for the next twenty years the real influence who can address himself to this."[15] The revolutionary doctrine, thus stated, is of prime importance in understanding Arnold's thought on political and social matters. It will be necessary later to trace the inner source from which the doctrine came.

Now an aristocracy, Arnold said, quite unlike the masses, is inherently unsusceptible to ideas; but it is acutely sensible to "considerations of policy, of respect for established facts, or compromise." And the English aristocracy, admirable as it is and has been, is no exception. Arnold had now arrived at a statement of his second major thesis, a corollary of the first and one of the cardinal tenets of his political and social position:

Members of an aristocracy, forming more or less a caste, and living in a society of their own, have little personal experience of the effect of ideas upon the masses of the people. They run little chance of catching the influence of these ideas by contact. On the other hand, an aristocracy has naturally a great respect for the established order of things, for the *fait accompli*. It is itself a *fait accompli*, it is satisfied with things as they are, it is, above everything, prudent. Exactly the reverse of the masses, who regard themselves as in a state of transition, who are by no means satisfied with things as they are, who are, above everything, adventurous. ... In general, an aristocracy is not sympathetic to ideas; it regards them as visionary, because it has not experienced them; and as dangerous, because they are independent of existing facts.[16]

These passages from *England and the Italian Question* mark the first statement of concepts essential to an understanding of Arnold's personal outlook and, above all, to a comprehension of his ideas on social and educational affairs. Here, it is true, the concepts have a political orientation. The characteristic insensibility of the British aristocracy to ideas, particularly to the ideas of revolutionary France, had led them to overestimate the results of their own victory of 1815; they had thought to destroy, to extirpate, the Revolution itself by negotiating the Treaties of Vienna; and having concluded that questionable peace, they had wishfully settled down to enjoy the old equilibrium, serenely assured that the Revolution no longer existed.

Louis Napoleon, on the other hand, had fully understood the temper

15 Super, v, 228.
16 *England and the Italian Question* (Super, I, 83). Cp. *The Popular Education of France* (Super, II, 11–15); and *Culture and Anarchy* (Super, v, 124–7).

of the French populace. He recognized its strong natural solicitude for the oppressed Italian people, its sympathetic yearning for freedom and liberty, to be seized as a gift and bestowed as a boon upon a sister nation. He knew that the French people would never have supported a war of conquest, that this "vast peasant proprietary" had but one desire – "to enjoy, in quiet and stability, its possession of the soil of France." And all this the Emperor knew because of a "positive element in his character which makes him unapt to be out of sympathy with the masses of the people. It is an element which he has repeatedly manifested in his writings, his speeches, and his actions. It is the most interesting feature of his character. It is his great advantage over the kings and aristocracies of Europe. *It is that he possesses, largely and deeply interwoven in his constitution, the popular fibre.*"[17]

In this, Arnold's first essay on political matters, there appears also a brief statement of another important premise: the natural antipathy of the British people – the aristocracy as well as the lower orders – to absolute government. It is well to remember that in 1859, in his first preoccupation with political affairs, Arnold was already cognizant of the one insuperable barrier to progress toward a comprehensive national system of schools, that is, the extreme misapprehension of the people concerning the one means by which their educational emancipation might be achieved – the benevolent intervention of the state. Ten years later, in *Culture and Anarchy* (1869), the same theme rises to a definitive protest; in *England and the Italian Question*, Arnold cites it merely as one reason for British misjudgment of Louis Napoleon. The English regard the Emperor, Arnold said, as a skilful despot who has mastered France and dealt with it for his own advantage. Consulting only the *élite* society of Paris, they have failed to discover the true, dominant popular opinion of the French industrial classes: that Louis Napoleon is "a beneficent ruler on whom they have themselves conferred power, and who wields it for the advantage of the French nation."[18]

17 Super, I, 81. (The italics are Arnold's.) In a letter of 22 May 1859, written from Nismes to his sister, Mrs. Forster, Arnold enlarges on this theme (see *The Unpublished Letters of Matthew Arnold*, ed. Arnold Whitridge, New Haven, 1923, pp. 43–9). Speaking seventeen years later (1876) before the London clergy at Sion College, Arnold quoted Ernest Renan: " 'Here is the great lesson of this history for our age; the times correspond to one another; the future will belong to that party which can get hold of the popular classes and elevate them' " ("The Church of England," *Last Essays on Church and Religion, The Works of Matthew Arnold*, Ed. de Luxe, London, 1904, IX, 361–2, hereafter designated as *Works*, Ed. de Luxe).

18 Super, I, 76.

One other important concept may be distinguished in *England and the Italian Question*, one that has already been noticed in the early letters: Arnold's admiration for the French people, with their sensitivity and their delight in ideas:

It is to the honour of France, it is what distinguishes her from all other nations, that the mass of her population is so accessible to considerations of this elevated order. It is the bright feature of her civilisation that her common people can understand and appreciate language which else-where meets with a response only from the educated and refined classes. One is tempted to ask oneself what would the French nation be if the general knowledge equalled the general intelligence. At present the accessibility to ideas, in France, is only equalled by the ignorance of facts.[19]

Here, in this last statement, Arnold was feeling for his anchor again; he was, after all, on an educational, and not a political, mission. In dealing with the political counterpart, however, he had developed four concepts important for understanding his social and educational theories and important also for an approach to *Culture and Anarchy*: (1) the grow-ing power of the popular will in shaping the destiny of nations; (2) the enforced abdication of an effete aristocracy, conservatively opposed to change and unsusceptible to ideas; (3) the antipathy of the English people to strong governmental intervention in social, economic, or political matters; and (4) the intellectual vigour of the French people, whose schools Arnold had come to observe.

THE REPORT ON THE SCHOOLS OF THE CONTINENT

In his formal report submitted to the Newcastle Commission[20] after his return from the Continent, Arnold first traced the history of elementary education in France. Quite in accord with the rumours frequently echoed in Parliament, he had found that a truly national system of schools already existed in France and that it was far superior in organiza-tion and scope of service to the amorphous and chaotic structure which

19 *Ibid.*, pp. 78–9.
20 *Reports of the Assistant Commissioners Appointed to Inquire into the State of Popular Education in Continental Europe and on Educational Charities in England and Wales* (London, 1861) IV, 13–160. Published separately by Arnold at his own risk as *The Popular Education of France* (Super, II).

then prevailed in England. Arnold's genius for systematic exposition prompted him naturally, not only to describe what he saw, but to account for so amazing a phenomenon as a sound national system, produced and perfected by a country so volatile and protean in its forms of government since the Revolution of 1789. France, he believed, despite its revolutionary passion for popular freedom, had, *through the instrumentality of strong, centralized, autocratic government,* created and perfected an educational structure which should be the envy of the British people.

The French educational system, Arnold explained, was basically of nineteenth-century growth. The Revolution itself had contributed little more than to establish the direction that the organization should take: "It made it impossible for any government of France to found a system which was not *lay,* and which was not *national.*" It was to the sagacity of the first Napoleon, Arnold said, that the centralized control and national unity of the structure were attributable.[21] Addressing himself to the most urgent problem of the moment, the rehabilitation of the secondary schools, the French Consul had promulgated the law of 1802, which had founded the educational system of the richer classes as it still existed when Arnold saw it in 1859. Primary education, however, had languished until the law of 1833 had founded a truly national elementary school system. The governing authority of the system had, nevertheless, been already created. By the law of 1806, Napoleon had instituted the Imperial University of France, which, under a hierarchy of grand master, councillors, inspectors-general, and rectors, was to administer the whole instruction of the nation, including the *lycées,* the communal colleges, and the primary schools. By a decree of 17 March 1808, it was established that "No school, no establishment of instruction whatsoever, can be formed outside the pale of the University, and without the authorization of its chief." Under the subsequent attacks of the clergy, of the Orleanists, and of the jealous successive governments, the University had been unable to maintain its exclusive supervisory control. The principles, however, of centralization, of permanence of control, of perpetuity of aims and spirit, were not to be entirely lost upon the

21 Arnold's frank admiration of Napoleon Bonaparte introduces an interesting critical problem. It should be remembered that he is speaking at a time when the phobias of the English people, aroused during the Revolution and the wars of the Consulate, still persisted in a vigorous quixotic form. It is clear that Arnold speaks here in deliberate disregard of what he knows is still a great national bogey, now re-animated by the French-Sardinian Campaign and centred apprehensively upon the ambitious figure of Louis Napoleon.

people. The concept of a national system came as naturally to the French popular mind, Arnold said, as the habitual jealousy and mistrust of state control had come to the British. Accordingly, the French authorities had moved with alacrity to provide the necessary legislative support of the educational institutions.

As early as February 1816, the Restoration Government of France had issued an ordinance providing a grant of £2000 from the national treasury for the provision of schoolbooks and model schools, and of recompense for deserving teachers. The ordinance had also established "cantonal committees" – veritable local school boards – "to watch over the discipline, morality, and religious instruction of primary schools." It had instituted, moreover, a teachers' certificate of three degrees, to be obtainable by examination before the rector's deputy. It had established a substantial measure of religious toleration by making special provision for the schools of the Protestant minority.

It was the law of 1833, however, that had established French education upon a firm and substantial footing.[22] At the base of the structure was a minimal elementary programme, including – besides moral and religious instruction and the basic rudiments of reading, writing, and arithmetic – the elements of French grammar and the French legal system of weights and measures. But beyond this basic training lay a provision for "superior primary instruction," designed for that large class of French artisans needing something more than the indispensable minimum, but not needing the classical Latin or Greek. The superior programme did not embrace foreign languages, ancient or modern, but it did comprehend "all that constitutes what may be called a good French education."

Complete freedom to institute and to maintain private schools was guaranteed by the law of 1833, but an effectual safeguard of the quality of instruction was demanded by the state, namely, the possession, by the teacher, of a certificate of capability. But lest the providing of schools should follow the natural, unequal distribution of wealth over the land (as it had done in England), the law of 1833 required every commune, either by itself or in conjunction with other adjacent communes, to

22 This was the year in which the British House of Commons had approved its first grant of £20,000 for the support of education through the sponsorship of the two school societies. In France the grant for primary education had risen to £28,000 in 1831, and to £40,000 in 1832. It would be thirty-seven more years before the British Parliament would approve a comparable education measure.

maintain at least one elementary school. To this school, or these schools, all the children of the communes were to be admitted, including the children of indigents, who might attend without paying any fees. In matters of religious instruction, the wishes of the parents were to be ascertained and followed in all that concerned their children's welfare.

The administration and supervision of the elementary schools of France were to be vested in two committees: the parish committee supplied by the commune and the district committee supplied by the *arrondissement*. In both of these committees the lay element predominated. To the communal, or parish, committee was delegated the inspection and superintendence of the schools; to the district, *comité d'arrondissement*, was confided the nomination of the teacher, as well as his dismissal, subject to the right of appeal to the Minister in Council.

The results of the law of 1833, Arnold said, were prodigious. The thirteen normal schools existent in that year increased to seventy-six within five years (1838), with more than 2,500 students in training. In four years, from 1834 to 1838, some 4,557 public schools were added to the 10,316 which had existed previously. The number of boys' schools had increased in thirteen years from 33,695 (in 1834) to 43,514 (in 1847), and the number of pupils increased over the same period from 1,654,828 to 2,176,079. By 1835, primary inspectors, "those 'sinews of public instruction,' " were permanently established by royal ordinance, one for each department. By 1847, two inspectors-general and 153 inspectors and sub-inspectors had been appointed. As a result of this remarkable expansion, by 1851, out of 37,000 communes of France, only 2,500 were still without schools.[23]

With the early defeat of the Revolution of 1848, a commission was appointed to report to the Ministry on the state of primary instruction throughout the country, and especially on the effects of the law of 1833. The law of 15 March 1850, which Arnold found still governing public education in France, was substantially based on the report of this commission. The law of 1850 abolished both the communal and the district committees and gave to the mayor and the minister of religion the supervision and moral direction of primary instruction in each commune. The committees were replaced by a new body made up of delegates from each canton (a division larger than the commune but smaller than the *arrondissement*). The delegates were nominated by the departmental council, a body which met twice a month at the chief town of each department. The departmental council consisted of thirteen members,

23 *The Popular Education of France* (Super, II, 72–3).

all nominated by the Minister of Education – that is, all except the prefect, the *procureur-général*, the bishop, and an ecclesiastical nominee of the bishop, who were members *ex officio*. Under the Second Empire, the departmental council nominated both the cantonal delegates and the commissions charged with the certification of teachers; it regulated the public primary schools, fixed the rate of school fees, drew up the lists of eligible teachers, judged the teachers in matters of discipline, and held the power to "interdict them absolutely and for ever from the exercise of their profession," subject to an appeal to the Imperial Council of Public Instruction in Paris. The Imperial Council was the central governing body; its members were appointed annually by the Emperor. "Before this council, the Minister, if he thinks fit, brings for discussion projected laws and decrees on public education. He is bound to consult it respecting the programmes of study, methods, and books, to be adopted in public schools. To watch in the provinces over the due observance of its regulations on these matters is the business of the rectors and their academic councils. Finally, the Imperial Council has to hear and judge the appeals of teachers on whom the departmental councils have laid their interdict."[24]

Such was the educational structure which Arnold, fresh from the chaos of British conflict and mismanagement, had discovered in the France of that crafty autocrat, Napoleon III. Even the religious conflict had been happily adjusted, though the policy of "comprehensive" instruction had been abandoned for one of segregation according to faiths. The earlier law of 1833, fathered by a wise Minister of Education, François Pierre Guizot, had tended to make denominational schools the exception, and common schools the rule. This provision, however, had proved not to satisfy perfectly the religious loyalties of the French people; accordingly, the law of 1850 was directed toward providing denominational schools. In those communes where more than one of the forms of worship recognized by the state (Catholicism, Protestantism, and Judaism) were professed, each form was to have its own separate school. The departmental councils might, where necessary, authorize the education of children of different faiths within a common school, but in such cases the religious liberty of all groups must be sedulously guarded.

Arnold's pronouncement on these tolerant protections is significant, for it reflects for the first time his own judgment on a perplexing social problem; it reveals, too, a temperament congenial to urbanity in social action:

24 *Ibid.*, pp. 80–1.

I confidently affirm, in contradiction to much ignorant assertion, that the liberty thus proclaimed by the law is maintained in practice. The venerable chiefs of the principal Protestant communities of the French provinces – the president of the Consistory of Nismes, the president of the Consistory of Strasbourg – individually assured me, that, as regarded the treatment of their schools by the authorities, they had nothing whatever to complain of; that Protestant schools came into collision with the authorities no otherwise than as Catholic schools came; that such collision, when it happened, was, in nine cases out of ten, on matters wholly unconnected with religion.[25]

Surely, in such a commentary, Arnold was looking critically toward home; he was urging indirectly upon the English people the essential tenor of his own belief, that this hitherto insuperable obstacle to educational progress in England could be resolved, and that here, in the France of the autocratic Second Empire, was the positive evidence thereof.

SECONDARY EDUCATION AND A FRENCH ETON

Arnold learned one other edifying lesson in France. He had gone to study elementary education, but he could not confine himself to such a limitation. Still more germane to his own immediate interest was another institution, the French secondary school, represented by the *lycée* and the communal college. " ... yet to touch on it for one moment in passing I cannot forbear," he said. And he added by way of apology: "I saw something of it; I inquired much about it; had I not done so, I should have comprehended the subject of French primary instruction very imperfectly." In the 63 *lycées* and the 244 communal colleges of France, Arnold found what he believed to be the proper model for British middle-class education: an institution "inspected by the State, aided by the State, drawing from this connection with the State both efficiency and dignity; and to which, in concert with the State, the departments, the communes, private benevolence, all co-operate to provide free admission for poor and deserving scholars."[26]

Arnold conceived of the secondary school as a leveller of class distinctions. Here again is one of his great intellectual convictions, a concept that is to become one of the cornerstones of *Culture and Anarchy*. His

25 *Ibid.*, p. 85.
26 *Ibid.*, p. 87.

statement of it is so important to an understanding of his central philosophy that it must be quoted at length:

Our middle classes are nearly the worst educated in the world. But it
is not this only; although, when I consider this, all the French commonplaces about the duty of the State to protect its children from the
charlatanism and cupidity of individual speculation seem to me to be
justified. It is far more than a great opportunity is missed of fusing all
the upper and middle classes into one powerful whole, elevating and
refining the middle classes by the contact, and stimulating the upper. In
France this is what the system of public education effects; it effaces
between the middle and upper classes the sense of social alienation; it
raises the middle class without dragging down the upper; it gives to
the boy of the middle class the studies, the superior teaching, the proud
sense of belonging to a great school, which the Eton or Harrow boy has
with us; it tends to give to the middle class precisely what they most
want, and their want of which is the great gulf between them and the
upper; it tends to give them personal dignity.[27]

In this passage Arnold has stated his doctrine of cultural fusion. By the
power of education, the contending social classes could be brought together, united by a common sympathy for the sharing of a common
destiny. The doctrine was not entirely hypothetical; already Arnold had
witnessed the beginnings of such a fusion. The professional classes of
England, the clergy and the barristers – all, in fact, who had enjoyed
the benefit of the great public schools – were already "nearly identified
in thought, feeling, and manners with the aristocratic class." But they
had bought their privilege at too great a price; the cost of such an education lay well beyond the ability of all but the affluent to pay. Either
most of the middle class must remain in its present deplorable condition
of ignorance and vulgarity, or the state must create institutions for its
nurture – "honourable because of their public character, and cheap because nationally frequented." The nation must choose between these
two alternatives. "If the former happens, then this great English middle
class, growing wealthier, more powerful, more stirring every year, will
every year grow more and more isolated in sentiment from the professional and artistocratic classes. If the latter, then not only will the
whole richer part of our rich community be united by the strong bond

27 *Ibid.*, p. 88. See also the passage from *Reports on Elementary Schools* (pp.
19–20), quoted in chap. I, p. 7.

of a common culture, but the establishment of a national system of instruction for the poorer part of the community will have been rendered infinitely easier."[28]

In this statement Arnold has drawn toward an explanation of his present digression from the major purpose of his mission abroad, the study of elementary education. The nation, he said, cannot have the one without the other. Already the parliamentary spokesmen of the English middle class had begun to complain that the poor were better provided for than their own people. Any attempt to increase the facilities of elementary instruction without some reciprocal provision on their behalf would arouse even greater discontent and opposition. Herein, Arnold believed, lay a great opportunity for the Newcastle Commission: "The Education Commissioners would excite, I am convinced, in thousands of hearts a gratitude of which they little dream, if, in presenting the result of their labours on primary instruction, they were at the same time to say to the Government, 'Regard the necessities of a not distant future, and *organise your secondary instruction.*' "[29]

In *Culture and Anarchy* Arnold was later to declare what he conceived to be the one best hope for British national regeneration.

The whole scope of the essay is to recommend culture as the great help out of our present difficulties; culture being a pursuit of our total perfection by means of getting to know, on all the matters which most concern us, the best which has been thought and said in the world; and through this knowledge, turning a stream of fresh and free thought upon our stock notions and habits, which we now follow staunchly but mechanically, vainly imagining that there is a virtue in following them staunchly which makes up for the mischief of following them mechanically. This, and this alone, is the scope of the following essay. And the culture we recommend is, above all, an inward operation.[30]

As he announced his thesis, his eye was fixed apprehensively upon the British Philistine, who now stood possessed of the nation's destiny – that "wild ass alone by himself," arrogantly and ignorantly out of contact "with the main current of national life"; an "incomplete and mutilated man," with a "natural taste for the bathos," a "want of sensitivity of intellectual conscience, a disbelief in right reason, a dislike of authority";

28 *Ibid.*, p. 89.
29 *Ibid.*, pp. 89–90.
30 *Culture and Anarchy* (Super, v, 233–4).

a man preoccupied with his "cartloads of rubbish," his "hole-and-corner forms of religion," his morbid concern for the right of "marriage with a deceased wife's sister," his querulous insistence upon the unbounded right to do exactly as he pleases.

With a genius for moderation and the constructive approach, Arnold faced this monstrous actuality and declared: "*This man does not deserve to be ousted; ousted he will not be, but transformed.*" Studying the French educational system, Arnold beheld the instrument of the Philistine's transformation – an ample provision of good secondary schools, bestowing knowledge, pride, and personal dignity; "honourable because of their public character, and cheap because nationally frequented."

The corollary, appearing also in these passages from *The Popular Education of France* (1861), deserves re-emphasis – namely, the cultural amalgamation of contiguous classes – the fusion of the middle with the upper "into one powerful whole, elevating and refining the middle classes by the contact, and stimulating the upper." Many years later Arnold was, with some trepidation,[31] to urge this theory upon the workingmen themselves – again on behalf of the middle class, and for the same reason: that in lending their suport to a national movement toward the development of secondary education, they might minister to the needs of a class to which they themselves might hope to rise and to which they themselves might be assimilated.[32] In *Culture and Anarchy* the idea recurs amid Arnold's analysis of the three great classes at the point where their distinctive appellations – *Barbarians, Philistines, Populace* – are bestowed:

It is obvious that that part of the working class which, working diligently by the light of Mrs. Gooch's Golden Rule, looks forward to the happy day when it will sit on thrones with commercial members of Parliament and other middle-class potentates, to survey, as Mr. Bright beautifully says, "the cities it has built, the railroads it has made, the manufactures it has produced, the cargoes which freight the ships of the greatest mercantile navy the world has ever seen," – it is obvious, I say, that this part of the working class is, or is in a fair way to be, one in spirit with the industrial middle class. It is notorious that our middle-class Liberals have long looked forward to this consummation,

31 *Letters*, ii, 150–2 (Monday, January 1879).
32 An address delivered to the Ipswich Working Men's College: "Ecce, Convertimur ad Gentes," *Fortnightly Review*, xxv, N.S. (1 Feb. 1879), 238–52; republished in *Irish Essays*, 1882 (*Works*, Ed. de Luxe, xi).

when the working class shall join forces with them, aid them heartily to carry forward their great works, go in a body to their tea-meetings, and, in short, enable them to bring about their millennium.[33]

In such a passage there scintillates, of course, the cynical humour so often found in Arnold, but it would be a mistake to underestimate therefore the serious meaning of his thought. Arnold was framing here a forecast of the British educational renaissance, and he had seen in France the means of its consummation, the state-supported secondary school. Accordingly, while on his tour of the Continent, though committed to the study of elementary education, he had seized every opportunity afforded him by the functionaries of government to visit and examine the *lycée* and the *collège*. And later, when after 1862 the tumult over the "Revised Code" had lifted, it was to the secondary school, to his *A French Eton*, that he turned as the object of his next endeavour.[34] The materials for that later effort, he had gathered in 1859, while serving on the Newcastle Commission. In May of that year, Arnold had visited the *lycée* at Toulouse; and from Toulouse he had travelled by coach over the Montagne Noire to the little village of Sorèze, the seat of the college instituted and still administered by Jean Baptiste Lacordaire. Here in the monastic quiet of an old abbey, Arnold had conversed with the great religious teacher, a friend of, and cosufferer with, Charles de Montalembert, and gathered the substance for *A French Eton*.[35]

In this work, Arnold described the French secondary system that had so favourably impressed him – the chief town of every French department with its *lycée*, the considerable towns of every department, each with its communal college: the *lycées* founded and maintained by the state, with the aid of the department and the commune; the colleges founded and maintained by the commune, with aid from the state.[36]

33 Super, v, 142.
34 Many years later, in performing his last commission to study the elementary schools of the Continent in 1886, Arnold turned again, at the close of his report, to the old theme, and enjoined the government to "organize our secondary instruction": *Special Report on Certain Points Connected with Elementary Education in Germany, Switzerland, and France*, Great Britain, Parliament, House of Commons, Command Paper 4752 (London, 1886), LI, 25.
35 Published in three parts: 1. *Macmillan's Magazine*, VIII (September 1863), 353–62; 2. *ibid.*, IX (February 1864), 343–55; 3. *ibid.*, X (May 1864), 83–96.
36 *A French Eton* (Super, II, 266–7).

And England, languishing with her nine public schools, serving, at the almost prohibitive cost of £100 to £200 a year per pupil, the slight segment of the British middle class sufficiently opulent to afford them! "Why," exclaims Arnold, "why cannot we have throughout England ... schools where the children of our middle and professional classes may obtain ... an education of as good quality, with as good guarantees, social character, and advantages for a future career in the world, as the education which French children of the corresponding class can obtain from institutions like that of Toulouse or Sorèze?"[37] Thwarted and abandoned through the dereliction of the British state, these seekers after learning, Arnold clearly saw, were plundered by the quacks and scoundrels of countless Dotheboys Halls, who flaunted their enticements, column by column, in the *Times*. And all this was provided, Arnold said ironically, "by the simple, natural operation of the laws of supply and demand, without, as the *Times* beautifully says, 'the fetters of endowment and the interference of the executive.' Happy country! happy middle classes! Well may the *Times* congratulate them with such fervency; well may it produce dithyrambs, while the newspapers of less-favoured countries produce only leading articles; well may it declare that the fabled life of the Happy Islands is already beginning amongst us."[38]

As for the natural law of supply and demand, to rely upon this principle in regulating the educational institutions of the nation was, Arnold said, "to lean upon a broken reed." The masses of mankind, who stood most in need of education, could not distinguish good teaching from bad; they knew not what they ought to demand, and if they did, they had no way of testing whether or not the required quality of instruction were being supplied to their children. There must be securities, Arnold insisted, such as the few great public schools of England provided by their publicity, by their wealth, importance, and connections, and by their reputation, which they must not forfeit. To these securities must be added another – supervision, which only the state can supply through regular, periodic inspection, together with the enforcement of definite minimal standards.[39]

As for the much-touted virtue of private enterprise and self-reliance in educating the children of the middle classes, Arnold contended that all other levels of tuition were already supported substantially by public grants: the universities and the public schools, existing primarily for the benefit of the artistocracy and the higher professional classes, enjoyed

37 *Ibid.*, p. 279.   38 *Ibid.*, pp. 281–2.   39 Ibid., pp. 282–3.

enormous endowments; the national schools for the poor were supported by state grants, and by parochial and national subscriptions. It was only the middle class that got nothing – that must shift for itself, glorying meanwhile in the false security of unfettered freedom from a bureaucratic control. How hollow, then, how vain, "how meaningless, to tell a man who, for the instruction of his offspring, receives aid from the State, that he is humiliated!" Arnold has come close again to one of the salient themes of *Culture and Anarchy*, the nature of the state as the personification of the citizen's best self:

Is a citizen's relation to the State that of a dependent to a parental benefactor? By no means; it is that of a member in a partnership to the whole firm. The citizens of a State, the members of a society, are really a partnership; "a partnership," as Burke nobly says, "in all science, in all art, in every virtue, in all perfection." Towards this great final design of their connexion, they apply the aids which co-operative association can give them. This applied to education will, undoubtedly, give the middling person a better schooling than his own individual unaided resources could give him; but he is not thereby humiliated, he is not degraded; he is wisely and usefully turning his associated condition to the best account.[40]

In *A French Eton* Arnold again turned the full power of his critical intellect upon that political anomaly, that social monstrosity, the British Philistine, who, in serene self-satisfaction with his own boorishness, would do nothing for himself educationally; who, in his jealous fears of governmental encroachments, would allow nothing to be done in his behalf; who, through such fuglemen as Roebuck and Baines, cried out his warped and arrogant prejudices in the *Times*: that "nobody has the same interest to do well for a man as he himself has," and that for the state to undertake such offices is to destroy those "habits of self-reliance" and to aim "a grievous blow at the independence of the English character."

It was the middle class, Arnold maintained, that had opposed and

40 *Ibid.*, p. 300. For a discussion of Arnold's possible sources for this concept in Carlyle's "Characteristics," see David J. DeLaura, "Arnold and Carlyle," *PMLA*, LXXIX (March 1964), 116. Echoes of Carlyle in Arnold's poetry are demonstrated by Kathleen Mary Tillotson, "Matthew Arnold and Carlyle" (Warton Lecture on English Poetry), *Proceedings of the British Academy* (London: Oxford University Press, 1956), pp. 133–53.

obstructed the benevolent action of the state. Traditionally identified with Nonconformity, embattled against the vested power of an ecclesiastical party, it had steadfastly refused to forget that "the hand that smote it – the hand which did the bidding of its High Church and prelatical enemies – was the hand of the State."[41] Descended from a Germanic line, the middle-class Englishman, Arnold complained, is cool to new ideas, and not easily ravished by them; he is not "a great enthusiast for universal progress," but he bears a strong love of discipline and order, "of keeping things settled, and much as they are"; he is worried by the actions of the onward-looking statesman and legislator, and is inclined "to act with bodies of men of his own kind, whose aims and efforts reach no further than his own." The middle class "has little turn for ideals; it is self-satisfied." It will have little to do with local government, relegating this function, if it is to be exercised at all, to the better-tempered aristocracy. How different from the well-ordered local management in France! "Every locality in France – that country which our middle class is taught so much to compassionate – has a genuine municipal government, in which the middle class has its due share; and by this municipal government all matters of local concern (schools among the number) are regulated; not a country parish in England has any effective government of this kind at all."[42]

In its former opposition to the state as the engine of the High Church party to persecute Nonconformists, the middle class, Arnold admitted, had wrought a noble work. "It rendered a valuable service to liberty of thought and to all human freedom." If the state now threatened to ally itself with a favoured faction, the middle class would do well to oppose it still. But the danger of such injustice, Arnold declared, has now been dissipated; the state shows more and more its resolution "to hold the balance perfectly fair between religious parties"; and if it does not, "the middle class has it in its own power, more than any other class, to confirm the State in this resolution. This class has the power to make it thoroughly sure – in organising, for instance, any new system of public instruction – that the State shall treat all religious persuasions with exactly equal fairness. If, instead of holding aloof, it will now but give its aid to make State-action equitable, it can make it so."[43]

Arnold had complete faith in the collective principle, in the creative

41 *A French Eton* (Super, II), p. 306.
42 *Ibid.*, pp. 306–7.
43 *Ibid.*, pp. 308–9.

power of concerted human beneficence, in "beneficence acting *by rule*," which was Burke's definition of law. He would only put the much-vaunted English self-reliance and love of individual action to better use by enlisting them in the service of a powerful, but still voluntary, organization. "Is 'English self-reliance and independence' to be perfectly satisfied," he asks, "with what it produces already without this organization? In middle-class education it produces, without it, the educational home[44] and the classical and commercial academy. Are we to be proud of that? Are we to be satisfied with that? Is 'the greatness of this country' to be seen in that?"[45]

All that had been so far accomplished for British elementary education, Arnold insisted, had been by means of a concerted social power, turning for its instrument to state action. To Baines's complaint that elementary education was already beginning to improve when the government interfered with it, Arnold replied that "it was because we were all beginning to take a real interest in it, beginning to improve it, that we turned to Government – to ourselves in our corporate character – to get it improved faster ... We asked ourselves if we could not employ our public resources on this concern, if we could not make our beneficence act upon it by rule, without losing our 'habits of self-reliance,' without 'aiming a grievous blow at the independence of the English character.' We found that we could; we began to do it; and we left Mr. Baines to sing in the wilderness."[46]

Here, then, Arnold declared, was the opportunity for middle-class energy and ambition to perfect itself through the power of education; to acquire ideas, sympathy, culture. And for the seekers after this goodly pearl, there was but one sufficient price – state action, "beneficence working by rule." By its own will and persistent action, the middle class

---

44 He has in mind here institutions like Salem House in *David Copperfield* and Dotheboys Hall in *Nicholas Nickleby*. Sixteen years later he spoke of Salem House as typical of middle-class schools: "I have this year been reading *David Copperfield* for the first time. Mr. Creakle's school at Blackheath is the type of our ordinary middle class schools, and our middle class is satisfied that so it should be" (*Letters*, II, 184, 14 October 1880). In "The Incompatibles" (*The Nineteenth Century*, April and June 1881), he uses Salem House and the men that such schools turn out – men like Murdstone and Quinion – as the examples of all in British middle-class society that is so antithetical, so irritating, so loathsome to the refined and sensitive Irish nature (*Irish Essays, and Others, Works*, Ed. de Luxe, XI, 58 ff.).

45 *A French Eton* (Super, II, 310). Cp. *Culture and Anarchy* (Super, V, 154–5).

46 *A French Eton* (Super, II, 310–11).

must secure both the means and the end. The secondary schools of the land, the great public schools, were in the hands of the aristocracy. Why should that class extend its own benevolence? These schools were already sufficient for the education of its restricted numbers. Why should it create competing institutions and raise up contenders with its own children? Why should it "labour to endow another class with those great instruments of power – a public spirit, a free spirit, a high spirit, a governing spirit?" Why should it "do violence to that distaste for State-action, which, in an aristocratic class, is natural and instinctive, for the benefit of the middle class?"[47]

In *A French Eton*, the humanistic principles that underlay Arnold's educational philosophy, principles that coloured and conditioned the whole tenor of his intellectual life, received their first clear and systematic enunciation. The basic tenet of the humanistic position is a belief in the perfectibility of man; and it was this luminous prospect that Arnold here revealed and delineated. But in the perfecting of the nation, the benighted middle class, so rapidly augmenting its political control, must undertake its own educational regeneration; it must correct its intolerable *laideur*, its insularity; it must cease "being frightened at shadows."

They may keep (I hope they always will keep) the maxim that self-reliance and independence are the most invaluable of blessings, that the great end of society is the perfecting of the individual, the fullest, freest, and worthiest development of the individual's activity. But that the individual may be perfected, that his activity may be worthy, he must often learn to quit old habits, to adopt new, to go out of himself, to transform himself. It was said, and truly said, of one of the most unwearied and successful strivers after human perfection that have ever lived – Wilhelm von Humboldt – that it was a joy to him to feel himself modified by the operation of a foreign influence. And this may well be a joy to a man whose centre of character and whose moral force are once securely established. Through this he makes growth in perfection. Through this he enlarges his being and fills up gaps in it; he unlearns old prejudices and learns new excellences; he makes advance towards inward light and freedom. Society may use this means of perfection as well as individuals, and it is a characteristic (perhaps the best characteristic) of our age, that they are using it more and more.[48]

Human perfectibility through the pursuit of culture – "our total

47 *Ibid.*, p. 312.
48 *Ibid.*, pp. 312–13.

perfection by means of getting to know, on all the matters which most concern us, the best which has been thought and said in the world." These are the familiar phrases that are to reverberate, from this time forward, in much that Arnold will have to say. They echo throughout his next important essay, "The Function of Criticism at the Present Time"; they constitute, in fact, its salient message: "to make the best ideas prevail," "to know the best that is known and thought in the world, and by in its turn making this known, to create a current of true and fresh ideas," "to keep man from a self-satisfaction which is retarding and vulgarizing, to lead him to perfection, by making his mind dwell upon what is excellent in itself, and the absolute beauty and fitness of things."[49] What it is essential to note is that here, in the region of Arnold's practical thought, in his preoccupations with the work-a-day problems of middle-class education, he had apprehended one of the basic themes of *Culture and Anarchy*: "the best which has been thought and said in the world; and through this knowledge, turning a stream of fresh and free thought upon our stock notions and habits, which we now follow staunchly but mechanically, vainly imagining that there is a virtue in following them staunchly which makes up for the mischief of following them mechanically."[50] Already, in 1864, he had conceived the ideas of 1869, and had given them palpable form.

It is in looking abroad, to the resources of a foreign culture, Arnold said, that the enlargement of vision, the perfection of character, are best to be fulfilled, not in basely leaning on the comfortable commonplaces of endemic thought. Thus had Wilhelm von Humboldt sought for the enlargement of his moral force, and so was it true of contemporary France that the widest breach "is being made in the old French mind." The extraordinary increase in German and English books, "books the most unlike possible to the native literary growth of France," was pulling to pieces "old stock French commonplaces," and putting a bridle "upon old stock French habitudes." It was thus that France had seen the necessity of controlling her own excessive state action. "She will not, and should not, ... cry down her great Revolution as the work of Satan; but she shows more and more the power to discern the real faults of that Revolution, the real part of delusion, impotence, and transitoriness in

49 Super, III, 261–71 and *passim*. Arnold's lecture, "The Function of Criticism at the Present Time," was delivered from the Oxford Chair of Poetry on 12 October 1864, only five months after the publication of the last section of *A French Eton* in May. The lecture itself was published a month later in the *National Review* (see Super, III, "Critical and Explanatory Notes," p. 472).
50 *Culture and Anarchy* (Super, v, 233–4).

the work of '89 and of '91, and to profit by that discernment." In England the path of enlightenment was to be pursued, Arnold believed, in the opposite direction, in accepting more and more the service of the state, "in taking the State's hand."

State-action is not in itself unfavourable to the individual's perfection, to his attaining his fullest development. So far from it, it is in ancient Greece, where State-action was omnipresent, that we see the individual at his very highest pitch of free and fair activity. This is because, in Greece, the individual was strong enough to fashion the State into an instrument of his own perfection, to make it serve, with a thousand times his own power, towards his own ends. He was not enslaved by it, he did not annihilate it, but he used it.[51]

No longer, Arnold said, might the middle class look to the old aristocracy for political leadership. The condition of the old aristocracy in England was one of decadence; even its culture was not what it once had been. The public schools frequented by this class were now wanting in intellectual life; the old classical studies were no longer in vogue.[52] Oxford had become a place for "schoolboys" at their games.[53] In forsaking the

---

51 *A French Eton* (Super, II, 314). Frank J. W. Harding attributes much of this tendency to rely upon the benevolent power of the state to the influence of Arnold's father, Dr. Thomas Arnold (cf. *Matthew Arnold, the Critic, and France*, Genève, 1964, pp. 161 ff.). Louis Bonnerot not only confirms the agreement between father and son in this particular, but expands it into a sweeping intellectual affinity: "Son père est à l'origine de ses théories sur l'aristocratie et la démocratie, sur la Révolution française, sur la nécessité d'un système politico-religieux qui fonderait une église vraiment nationale et chrétienne, sur les dangers, pour l'Angleterre, du conservatisme et de l'isolement. Quand le Dr. Arnold déclare 'the characteristic faculties of the English mind, [are] narrowness of view, and a want of learning and a sound critical spirit', non seulement nous croyons lire une phrase de son fils, mais nous sentons combien, intellectuellement, le père et le fils étaient faits pour s'entendre." (*Matthew Arnold, Poète*, Paris, 1947, p. 18.)

52 In *Friendship's Garland* (1866) Arnold's cynical *alter ego*, Arminius, says: "When I was over in England the other day, my poor friend Mr. Matthew Arnold insisted, with his usual blind adoration of everything English, on taking me down to admire one of your great public schools; precious institutions, where, as I tell him, for £250 sterling a year your boys learn gentlemanly deportment and cricket" (Super, V, 52).

53 As the devil's advocate in *Friendship's Garland*, Arnold defended the classical education of Viscount Lumpington and the Rev. Esau Hittall against the cynical inquisitiveness of Arminius thus: " 'Were the minds of Lord Lumpington and Mr. Hittall much braced by their mental gymnastics?' inquired

classics, the scions of the old aristocracy had not even turned to a comparable literature of modern times; they no longer read Goethe and Montesquieu, but the *Times* and the *Agricultural Journal*. They merely amused themselves. The aristocratic class had lost its best power, the power of ideas.

Remembering Arnold's antipathy to the British Philistine, recalling the ardour and high seriousness with which he had contended against him, one is impressed by the urbanity and magnanimity of his final judgment:

It is the middle class which has the real mental ardour, real curiosity; it is the middle class which is the great reader; that immense literature of the day which we see surging up all round us, – literature the absolute value of which it is almost impossible to rate too humbly, literature hardly a word of which will reach, or deserves to reach, the future, – it is the middle class which calls it forth, and its evocation is at least a sign of a widespread mental movement in that class. Will this movement go on and become fruitful: will it conduct the middle class to a high and commanding pitch of culture and intelligence? That depends on the sensibility which the middle class has for *perfection*; that depends on its power to *transform itself*.[54]

"Its power to transform itself" – here again a cardinal concept of *Culture and Anarchy* is being enunciated. Hitherto, in its public action, the middle class had shown only "the power and disposition to affirm itself, not at all the power and disposition to *transform itself*." It had asserted its raw, rough, vulgar, egocentric self, and turned in scorn from any high-souled aspiration for perfection. It had been content "to esteem itself for what it is, to try to establish itself just as it is, to try even to impose itself with its stock of habitudes, pettinesses, narrownesses, short-comings of every kind, on the rest of the world as a conquering power."[55]

Before the middle class could come into its own, Arnold insisted, it must experience an immense transformation; it must be "liberalised by

---

Arminius. 'Well,' I answered, 'during their three years at Oxford they were so much occupied with Bullingdon and hunting that there was no great opportunity to judge. But for my part I have always thought that their both getting their degree at last with flying colours, after three weeks of a famous coach for fast men, four nights without going to bed, and an incredible consumption of wet towels, strong cigars, and brandy-and-water, was one of the most astonishing feats of mental gymnastics I ever heard of.' " (*Ibid.*, p. 70)

54 *A French Eton* (Super, ɪɪ, 316–17).
55 *Ibid.*, p. 317.

an ampler culture, admitted to a wider sphere of thought"; its provincialism must be dissipated, "its intolerance cured, its pettiness purged away." Then, let it rule. And for this transformation, this rebirth into a new dispensation, there was but one effectual means:

And I cannot see any means so direct and powerful for developing this great and beneficent power as the public establishment of schools for the middle class. By public establishment they may be made cheap and accessible to all. By public establishment they may give securities for the culture offered in them being really good and sound, and the best that our time knows. By public establishment they may communicate to those reared in them the sense of being brought in contact with their country, with the national life, with the life of the world; and they will expand and dignify their spirits by communicating this sense to them. I can see no other mode of institution which will offer the same advantages in the same degree.[56]

As has been stated, Arnold postponed the writing of *A French Eton* until the tumult over the "Revised Code" of 1862 had subsided sufficiently to release his attention to other things. This essay was not a part of his report to the Newcastle Commission; it represents, nevertheless, an excursion into a related field which Arnold could not dissociate from his precise commitment. For us, therefore, it stands in an integral relationship with his official report on the schools of the Continent, and to the two related essays: *England and the Italian Question* and "Democracy." It stands, moreover, along with these essays, in clear antecedent relationship to Arnold's definitive social essay, *Culture and Anarchy*. The important point to be noted is that Arnold, in his study of the politics and the education of the Continent, was laying block by block the foundation of his great pronouncement; that the origins of this work trace back to the professional thinking of the assistant commissioner and the lay inspector of schools. A categorical statement such as this must indeed have some limitation; a stream of intellect so broad, so various, so organically interwoven as Arnold's, would consist of many confluent elements not easily isolated or rechannelled once they were intermingled. The distinguishing characteristic of Arnold's thought is, in fact, the constant recurrence of salient strands, emphasized again and again, in one context and then another, but always with a gratifying pertinence, and always with a singularly unifying effect upon the whole body of his work. And so it is that anyone already familiar with the Prefaces and

56 *Ibid.*, pp. 322–3.

with the Oxford lectures will find in *Culture and Anarchy* the ever-present traces of consanguinity – the references to Sainte-Beuve, to Heine, and to Joubert; the pointing to the prevalent vulgarity, hideousness, ignorance, violence, as "really so many touchstones which try our one thing needful." There are also in *Culture and Anarchy* those evidences of doctrinal exegesis which anticipate unmistakably the main themes of the religious essays – the this-wordliness of St. Paul's meaning of the resurrection and the questionable credulity of the believers in miraculous revelation – themes which are later to be fully exploited in *St. Paul and Protestantism* (1870), in *Literature and Dogma* (1873), and in *God and the Bible* (1875).

There are, however, in the definitive essay of 1869,[57] certain strong, fundamental concepts which underlie the total thesis; and it is these that had their inception in Arnold's observations on the Continent. Stated succinctly, these are: (1) a belief in the silent, inarticulate, often inscrutable, but nevertheless prescient mind of the people, which presides as the real genius over social and political change; (2) a certainty of the lost predominance of a static, effete, and intellectually slumbrous aristocracy, deliberately incredulous of the mounting revolutionary currents and still trusting wishfully in an ancient *fait accompli*; (3) a conviction of the immense, the tragic, need for the enlightenment of the rising middle class, the new holder of the franchise, through the creation of a national system of public education, particularly secondary schools; (4) a determination to expose that mistaken, quixotic fear that the English people have of strong governmental institutions, which leads them to preclude, with their unreasoned obsession, the one action by which their own enlightenment might be fulfilled – the benevolent intervention of the state, the symbol of their collective better selves; and (5) a belief in the inevitable fusion of the social classes by a process of cultural assimilation, as the vehicle of the democratic consummation.

Unfortunately, when Arnold first uttered these idealistic principles, the educational renaissance for England was hardly imminent. Even as he spoke, the forces of reaction were brooding evil. A discussion of the direction of these forces, together with Arnold's vigorous endeavour to oppose them, will constitute the substance of the next chapter. Meanwhile it is fitting to remark that his fidelity to these principles, despite their stubborn rejection by his countrymen, reflects the dominant temper of his life and character – a steadfast holding to that which is good.

57 The parts of *Culture and Anarchy* were published previously in *The Cornhill Magazine* from July 1867 to August 1868.

III

"Payment by Results,"
An Example of
Philistine Polity

THE SCHOOLS AS THE AGENTS OF CULTURE AND GOOD TASTE

"Civilisation," said Arnold, "is the humanisation of man in society. Man is civilised when the whole body of society comes to live with a life worthy to be called *human*, and corresponding to man's true aspirations and powers." Among the means by which this happy state was to be attained, the familiar power of personal human expansion stood at the pinnacle of importance.[1] To achieve this end – the humanization of man in society – was the mission of the schools. And this was the purpose even of the elementary schools which he inspected.

Accordingly, in his very first report to the Committee of Council, Arnold deprecated the low degree of mental culture and intelligence exhibited by the pupil-teachers in contrast to their possession of facts.[2] Arnold clearly recognized the cause of this condition. Already his humanistic temperament had prompted him to distinguish the thing most needful as a civilizing agent, the literary record of man – not the dismal substitutes for it so universally offered in the schools. A surprising "knowledge of grammar, of the minutest details of geographical and historical facts, and above all of mathematics" had certainly failed to humanize the young candidates for the schoolmaster's career. If only they might have had portions of the best English authors and composition.

Throughout the whole series of his official reports, Arnold urged the addition of this genuine cultural influence. After his return from the Continent in 1860, he was prompted still to complain of the sterile reading books used in English schools:

1 "Preface," *Mixed Essays, Works*, Ed. de Luxe, x, vi.
2 *Reports on Elementary Schools* (London, 1889), pp. 19–20. Cp. p. 7, *supra*.

It is not enough remembered in how many cases his reading-book forms the whole literature, except his Bible, of the child attending a primary school. If then, instead of literature, his reading-book, as is too often the case, presents him with a jejune encyclopaedia of positive information, the result is that he has, except his Bible, no literature, no *humanising* instruction at all. ... I have seen school-books belonging to the cheapest, and therefore most popular series in use in our primary schools, in which far more than half of the poetical extracts were the composition either of the anonymous compilers themselves, or of American writers of the second and third order; and these books were to be some poor child's Anthology of a literature so varied and so powerful as the English! To this defectiveness of our reading-books I attribute much of that grave and discouraging deficiency in anything like literary taste and feeling, which even well-instructed pupil-teachers of four or five years' training, which even the ablest students in our training schools, still continue almost invariably to exhibit; a deficiency, to remedy which, the progressive development of our school system, and the very considerable increase of information among the people, appear to avail little or nothing.[3]

Schools were instituted, in Arnold's view, as the essential instruments of liberal culture and good taste, as the true disseminators of sweetness and light. Their best method, however, would be not to teach the rules of taste directly – "a lesson which we shall never get learnt" – but to diffuse "the best that has been thought and said in the world." Theirs was a *belletristic* function. The "recitation," for example, which was simply an exercise in memorizing and reciting passages of good poetry, would, he thought, instill more culture than the learning of rules, for, besides the direct discipline of learning something right, it had another, larger value: "out of the mass of treasures thus gained (and the mere process of gaining which will have afforded a useful discipline for all natures), a second and a more precious fruit will in time grow; they [the learners] will be insensibly nourished by that which is stored in them, and their taste will be formed by it, as the learning of thousands of lines of Homer and Virgil has insensibly created a good literary taste in so many persons, who would never have got this by studying the rules of taste."[4]

One is inclined to ponder the persistent faith in the power of letters Arnold so steadily maintained as he made the dreary round of the

3 *Ibid.*, pp. 87–8.
4 *Ibid.*, pp. 94–5.

schools, for nowhere was the effect to be observed. He spoke as from the prompting of an inner voice emerging out of his own experience. When he returned from the Continent, the doctrine stood as the one thing needful for his country's regeneration. Knowing these things, one is prepared to estimate the devastating shock he was about to suffer through the Philistine machinations of his own department under the measure known as "Payment by Results." This designation referred to the so-called Revised Code of Robert Lowe (later Viscount Sherbrooke), the new vice-president of the Committee of Council. If Arnold had begun to deprecate the mean hypocrisy and selfish opportunism of Philistine motives in legislative matters generally, here was an instance that touched him personally. Not only did Lowe's proposal tend to frustrate every semblance of cultural progress, every hope for the triumph of right reason, every promise of a new diffusion of sweetness and light, but it threatened to transform Arnold's own professional duties into a dull and stultifying clerkship. If he had been apathetic heretofore to the legislative matters that affected his own occupation, he was to turn now to the most vigorous personal intervention of his lifetime.

THE RECOMMENDATIONS OF THE NEWCASTLE COMMISSION

Both the testimony and the recommendations of the Newcastle Commission had pointed directly to the problems that Lowe sought to mitigate by his Revised Code. The facts are that the Commission itself had recommended a plan for simplifying the clerical burden of disbursement, and that this plan became the basic pattern for Lowe's proposed "Payment by Results." The commissioners had been convinced by the testimony of Ralph R. W. Lingen, secretary of the Committee of Council, that the dispensing machinery of the government had reached the utmost limits of manageability, and that either a simpler means of aiding the schools must be devised,[5] or the present cumbersome system would effectually obstruct all efforts to accommodate the vastly expanding needs of the nation.

The Commission had therefore proposed that all assistance given to the annual maintenance of schools should be simplified and reduced to grants of two kinds. The first grant would come entirely from state funds and would be paid upon the average attendance of the children during the year preceding the inspector's visit, "according to the opinion

5 Cf. Super, ii, 357, Note to 233: 2–4.

formed by the Inspectors of the discipline, efficiency, and general character of the school" – provided that a certificated teacher had been employed for nine calendar months. The second grant would come from county rates, and would depend upon the recommendation of a county examiner, a man to be chosen from among the ranks of the schoolmasters. It would be his duty to examine individually every child presented to him in reading, writing, and arithmetic. The managers of all schools fulfilling the conditions as specified would be entitled "to be paid out of the county rate a sum varying from 22s. 6d. to 21s. for every child who has attended the school during 140 days in the year preceding the day of examination, and who passes an examination before the county examiner in reading, writing, arithmetic, and who, if a girl, also passes an examination in plain needle work."[6]

The main advantage of the plan, it was alleged, would be the simplification of the system of distributing grants. Under this arrangement, the inspector would simply report to the Committee of Council the individual amounts payable to the schools in his district out of the "central" grant. The Committee of Council would thereupon send to the county and borough treasurers a statement of the amounts payable to the several schools within their areas. The sum total payable to all the schools in each county or borough would be transmitted to the treasurers in a lump, and would be disbursed by them in accordance with the schedule furnished by the Committee of Council.

The Newcastle Commission claimed for its plan several advantages besides the simplification of administrative machinery. For one thing, it promised some measure of relief for the schools in the more destitute places which could not at present qualify for the government grants because of their inability to match funds. Hereafter, should the plan receive parliamentary approval, this disability would be removed, and some premium might be paid upon every pupil who had given proof of having acquired a definite amount of knowledge. The plan seemed likely, also, to arouse local interest in education through the publication by local boards of examination results, and through the official reporting of the prevailing conditions which had affected the amount of the government grants payable to the local schools. The success of the pupils in the standard examinations would be likely, moreover, to direct a more critical scrutiny upon the management of the school and upon the quality of instruction.[7]

6 *Reports of the Commissioners*, 1, 328–30.
7 *Ibid.*, pp. 340–1.

In its deliberations on the report of the Newcastle Commission, the Committee of Council was aware of several options; it might accept the recommendations, or it might reject or adapt them. It evidently decided to adapt. The plan of the Committee was introduced in the House of Commons on 11 July 1861, apropos of an item of supply "to complete the sum necessary to defray the Charge for Public Education in Great Britain, to the 31st day of March, 1862." Robert Lowe, the vice-president of the Committee of Council,[8] commented upon the criticism which the Newcastle Commissioners had made on the operations of the department: "As I have taken down the charges brought against us, they are four in number: – First, the great expense of the present system; secondly, the defective instruction given under it; thirdly, its complexity; and fourthly, its inability to reach remote rural districts and the lower parts of towns."[9]

In order to deal with the defects which the Newcastle Commissioners had pointed out, Lowe announced the outline of a Minute shortly to be laid upon the table of the Commons which he hoped would alleviate the worst evils of the system. Briefly stated, the new plan would simplify the present payments to teachers and pupil-teachers by entrusting to the managers the distribution of the amounts due, rather than continuing the complicated system of personal payment by post office orders. Furthermore, the various grants to teachers and pupil-teachers, established by the Minutes of 1846,[10] would now be comprehended under a single capitation grant to be based upon attendance. The only qualification for payment of the grants would be that the school be provided with a certificated teacher and that it be certified by the inspector to be "in a fit state." Inspectors would examine the children in reading, writing, and arithmetic, and recommend the payment of one-third of the total grant for each child on his passing successfully in any one of the three subjects, the total grant being receivable if the child were successful in

8 An office created by act of Parliament in 1856 to provide an official liaison between the Committee of Council and the House of Commons. The vice-president of the Council must be "capable of being elected and of sitting and voting as a member of the House of Commons," with a salary not exceeding £2,000 per annum (*General Statutes, 19th and 20th Years of Queen Victoria*, London, 1856). W. F. Cowper (afterwards Cowper-Temple), the author of the clause to be known as "Cowper-Templeism" in the Education Act of 1870, was the first incumbent of this important office (Adams, pp. 224–5). See also Super, II, 348.

9 Hansard, Third Series, CLXIV, 721.

10 See Introduction, *supra*, pp. xviii–xx.

all three. "Our object is," said Lowe, "to secure, as far as possible, that the attention of the master shall not be confined to the upper class of his school, but shall be given to the whole, and we endeavour to effect that object by making the payment of the capitation grant depend upon the manner in which he has instructed each child."[11]

The Minute of Council was placed on the table of the Commons in the closing days of the session (29 July 1861). During the long recess it apparently stimulated widespread comment and discussion – so much, in fact, that the Committee felt impelled to revise it. On 13 February 1862, Lowe rose to announce that

These papers contained the projected amendments on the Revised Minute of the Regulations of the Committee of the Privy Council on Education. They form the result, as far as we are concerned, of six months' controversy. We have paid the greatest and most respectful attention to the opinions which have been ventilated by a number of very able gentlemen in pamphlets and in other ways; and being sincerely anxious to profit by the labours of those whose experience and ability enable them to judge the subject, we have endeavoured to make the Minute conform, as far as our sense of public duty will permit, to their views.[12]

In commenting upon the specific changes that the Committee of Council had felt impelled to make, Lowe called attention to the early age at which the great mass of the children of the poor ceased their education. On the average, 70 per cent of those in attendance were under ten years of age, 80 per cent were under eleven years, and 89 per cent under twelve years of age. Obviously these children were compelled by practical necessity to terminate their education thus early; if anything were to be done for them, it must be done in evening schools, where they might continue their learning after the day's work.[13]

The Committee of Council, therefore, had decided to do something for all the pupils, including those enrolled in evening schools, and to do it by the simple method of applying *a single grant entirely dependent on the results of an examination in reading, writing, and arithmetic* given by the inspector to each and every pupil above six years of age. It now proposed, said Lowe, that

11 Hansard, Third Series, CLXIV, 735.
12 *Ibid.*, CLXV, 191–2.
13 *Ibid.*, 208–10.

"The managers of schools may claim per scholar 1*d*. for every attendance
after the first 100 at the morning or afternoon meetings, and after the
first 12 at the evening meetings of their school. One third part of the
sum thus claimable is forfeited if the scholar fails to satisfy the Inspector
in reading, one-third if in writing, one-third if in arithmetic, respec-
tively."
That is the basis of our proposition. We do not make the grant upon
reading, writing, and ciphering, without attendance, because we
thought it quite possible that, if we did, children might be entered the
day before the examination, in order to pass for the grant. ... Then
we make rules for withholding the grant in certain cases – if the building
is not properly lighted, drained, and ventilated; if the teacher is not
duly certificated; if the registers are not kept with sufficient accuracy;
if the girls are not taught plain needlework; or if there are any gross
faults in the management of the school.[14]

It may easily be perceived that under Lowe's present proposal, the
principle of simplification approached the vanishing point. The whole
complicated system of dispensing aid to the schools would be reduced
to one single grant entirely dependent on an examination of the pupils
in reading, writing, and arithmetic. The scale of the devastation envisioned by the true devotees of popular education is difficult to estimate.
For one thing, the measure would sweep away the whole visible supporting structure of the normal schools, together with all pupil-teacher
subsidization, as established by the Minutes of 1846. By the provisions
of those Minutes, the Committee of Council had placed the training of
teachers upon a secure professional basis. It had given substantial guarantees for the improved status of the schoolmaster and had relieved, by
government subsidies, the hardships and insecurities which the occupation had traditionally entailed. It had also recognized the pressing need
for strengthening the normal schools that had sprung up since the
beginning of the century under the auspices of the two school societies.
It had sought to attract to them a more promising class of candidates
than had hitherto been enrolled. The principals of these normal schools
had formerly complained that their students had not been grounded in
ordinary elementary knowledge, that they lacked proper physical, mental, and moral qualifications. "It is reported that a great number of the
candidates and students of the Normal Schools show signs of scrofula,
and that generally their physical temperament is sluggish and inert.

14 *Ibid.*, 217.

They have too often had no further instruction than what can be obtained in an elementary school of average character, during the usual period of attendance, till 13 years of age."[15]

The complete reversal of the Committee of Council, apropos of teacher-training, since the remarkable improvements of 1846 is an amazing anomaly. For it was in the reduction of support for teacher-training that Lowe's Committee had determined most to economize. In its zeal for simplification, the Committee now proposed "to give an honorary certificate to every teacher who shall remain in a training college for two years. It will not have any pecuniary value,[16] but it will be a distinction, and may, we hope, operate in some degree to induce students to remain in the college for the longer period."[17] The "honorary certificate" – honorary, but to be given indiscriminately to all the candidates – was, in fact, a substitute for most of the extra inducements provided by the Minutes of 1846. The augmentation grants payable according to the degree of the certificate received, a portion of the Queen's Scholarships given on behalf of the pupil-teachers to the training colleges, and the extra fees to be earned by the schoolmasters for instructing pupil-teachers and monitors were all to be swept away.

There was an unmistakable note of sagacity in Lowe's statement of the case. To those who were apprehensive over curtailed programs and lost funds, he offered this specious reassurance:

I think there is no reason, therefore, for this apprehension with regard to loss. We know that there will be a loss where the teaching is inefficient. That is our principle, that where the teaching is inefficient the schools should lose. I cannot promise the House that this system will be an economical one, and I cannot promise that it will be an efficient one, but I can promise that it shall be either one or the other. If it is not cheap it shall be efficient; if it is not efficient it shall be cheap. The present is neither one nor the other. If the schools do not give instruction the public money will not be demanded, but if instruction is given the public money will be demanded – I cannot say to what amount, but the public will get value for its money.[18]

The subtle import was not lost upon the friends of popular education. Not since the institution of the Committee of Council in 1839 did an

---

15 Kay-Shuttleworth, *Four Periods of Public Education*, p. 480.
16 That is, the attractive "degrees of merit" would now be done away with (see Introduction, *supra*, pp. xix–xx.
17 Hansard, Third Series, CLXV, 221.
18 *Ibid.*, 229–30.

educational matter arouse such a vehement protest. Benjamin Disraeli arose to attack the motives of the vice-president. He warned the Commons that "we have now before us not only the Revised Code, but a Revision of the Revised Code.[19] We have, indeed, a new measure, abounding with details of a kind which requires the most careful scrutiny before we can arrive at any satisfactory conclusion upon them."[20]

Sir John Pakington, the father of the Newcastle Commission, urged moderation and a suspension of judgments until the whole matter could be given careful consideration in the Commons. He admitted surprise, however, "at the apparent inconsistency between the right hon. Gentleman's language to-night and that which he held during the last Session. I find that last Session, referring to the new Code which he was about to introduce, he said, 'It leaves the whole system of the Privy Council intact.' That language was not forgotten, and it was, I think, very much on account of it that the public mind was aroused and rendered somewhat indignant at finding laid on the table of the House at the extreme end of the Session a Code which was generally regarded as entirely upsetting the system of the Privy Council."[21]

ARNOLD'S OPPOSITION TO "PAYMENT BY RESULTS"

Four months after the Minute had been presented before Parliament, Matthew Arnold had decided to oppose it actively. On 13 November 1861, he wrote to his mother:

I am taking one or two of the spare days left me to begin either my lecture or my article on the Code. I do not quite know whether I will not put off the latter till January's *Fraser*. Shuttleworth has just published a most important pamphlet, and it is said that the Dean of Hereford, Dawes, is preparing an answer. Derwent Coleridge, too, is said to have a pamphlet in the press, and my object is rather to sum up the controversy, to give the general result of the whole matter, and to have the last word. My disinclination to begin anything has, however,

19 The first Code was a compilation in 1855 of all the former Minutes issued by the Committee of Council. A later compilation, prepared in 1860 during the vice-presidency of Robert Lowe, came to be known as "The Original Code" because its division of the regulations into chapters and articles became the model for all future codes (Sir Henry Craik, *The State in Its Relation to Education*, London, 1884, pp. 65–6; see also Binns, pp. 267–8).
20 Hansard, Third Series, CLXV, 243.
21 *Ibid.*, 254.

I daresay, a large share in my disposition to put off the thing for a month. In the meantime I begin neither the article nor the lecture, and the next fortnight I shall have a bad time of it, I suspect. Shuttleworth's pamphlet is most effective. You should order it – it costs a shilling. For the general reader and for members of Parliament there is a little too much detail, and the matter is hardly enough treated in its first principles for my taste, but for the large body of persons who have a finger in schools for the poor it is just the thing. It sells like wild-fire. One Educational Society alone, the Wesleyan, has taken a thousand copies, and the Educational Societies jointly are sending a copy to every member of both Houses of Parliament. Shuttleworth tells me the printer can hardly print them fast enough.[22]

Arnold humoured his disinclination to begin. He put off the writing of his article until January in order to complete his Homer lecture,[23] but on 19 February 1862, just six days after Lowe's speech before the Commons, he had already corrected the proofs. Again he wrote to his mother:

I have just finished correcting the proofs of my article for *Fraser*, and, what is harder, retouching and adding as was necessary. It will be very long, but I think not dull. Lowe's attack on the inspectors quite relieved me from all scruples in dealing with him, and I think my comments on his proceedings will be found vivacious. As to the article making a *sensation*, that I by no means expect. I never expect anything of mine to have exactly the popular quality necessary for making a sensation, and perhaps I hardly wish it. But I daresay it will be read by some influential people in connexion with the debate which will soon come on. Froude's[24] delay has certainly proved not unfortunate, as the present is a more critical moment for the article to appear than the beginning of the month, when Lowe's concessions were not answered, and could not be discussed.[25]

Anyone cognizant of Arnold's former reticence in criticizing the judgment of his superiors on the Committee of Council will be amazed at

22 *Letters*, I, 150 (November 13, 1861).
23 *On Translating Homer: Last Words* (1862) (Super, I, 168–216). See *Letters*, I, 153 (20 November 1861).
24 James Anthony Froude (1818–94), the eminent historian, had succeeded J. W. Parker (deceased) as editor of *Fraser's Magazine* in 1860, a position he continued to fill for fourteen years (*Dictionary of National Biography*).
25 *Letters*, I, 158 (February 19, 1862).

the vigour of his attack upon the Revised Code. Froude's delay had indeed proved advantageous, for Arnold was reading the proofs for the article just as the tumult flared over Lowe's announcement of a radical revision of the former Minute.

Taking Shuttleworth's pamphlet[26] at his *point de départ*, Arnold explained the need of a simpler statement for the general public and announced his intention to prepare one – "a statement dealing less with the details of the subject and more with its *rationale*."[27] He proposed to show the general reader, "at this last moment before the Parliamentary discussion comes 1. What it is that the Revised Code will actually do; 2. Why its authors are trying to do this; 3. What is the merit of their design in itself, and what, moreover, is the prospect of its accomplishing what it intends." And he proposed, in conclusion, to consider the recent "changes in his original scheme which have just been propounded by Mr. Lowe, and examine the value and importance of these."[28]

First of all, Arnold said, the Revised Code might be expected to reduce the grants currently contributed by the state for the education of the poor. Shuttleworth had estimated the loss at two-fifths of the present amount, or £175,000 a year; and this Arnold considered a reasonable estimate. At the prospect of such a reduction, he said, the old friends of state support were dismayed and discouraged; while the bitter adversaries of the system, the Voluntaryists and the industrial conservatives, were as much surprised as rejoiced. " 'It is a step in the right direction,' says Mr. Miall.[29] 'The penny will become a halfpenny, the halfpenny will become a farthing, and the farthing nothing at all.' "[30] As Shuttleworth had said in his pamphlet, it was difficult to understand why a department of state should recommend a course which actually threatened its own existence. Arnold's comment on the anomaly was that "the

26 "Letter to Earl Granville, k.g., on the Revised Code of Regulations Contained in the Minute of the Committee of Council on Education Dated July 29th, 1861," Kay-Shuttleworth, *Four Periods of Public Education*, pp. 574–638.

27 "The Twice-Revised Code," *Fraser's Magazine*, LXV (March 1862), 347–65; Super, II, 213.

28 *Ibid.*

29 Edward Miall, prominent Dissenter and Voluntaryist; editor of the *Nonconformist*, a weekly publication whose motto, "The Dissidence of Dissent and the Protestantism of the Protestant Religion," Arnold often ridiculed; member of Parliament for Rochdale from 1852 to 1857; and a member of the Newcastle Commission, which reported in 1861 (*Dictionary of National Biography*).

30 Super, II, 214.

secretary who drew up the new Code should have been Mr. Miall; the vice-president who defended it should have been Mr. Baines."[31]

The second point Arnold proposed to discuss involved the motives of the authors of the Revised Code. It was here that he found himself most personally concerned; for the aim of the framers of the Minute had placed in clear juxtaposition the absurd economy of the Philistine statesmen, on the one hand, and the cultural ideals which he most cherished, on the other. The penny-wise manipulators in the government, Arnold cynically complained, would reduce the educational responsibilities of the state to a strict limitation: " 'The duty of a State in public education is,' it is said, 'when clearly defined, to obtain the greatest possible quantity of reading, writing, and arithmetic for the greatest number.' These are, so far as the State is concerned, 'the education of the people.' To obtain the greatest possible quantity of these is 'the requirement of a State;' ... To give this is 'the one thing which the elementary schools of the State are bound to do, just as the one thing a brewer is bound to do is to make good beer.' "[32]

Arnold's ironical tone is now rising sharply. He continues in this vein by ridiculing the complaints of these penurious men that the state has attempted to give more than the beginning of rudimentary knowledge and paid for other things – "for discipline, for civilisation, for religious and moral training, for a superior instruction to clever and forward children – all of them matters quite out of its province ..." It has not restricted its grants to first things. "While inspectors were reporting on the tone and general influence of a school, on the discipline and behaviour of the children, on the geography and history of the first class, the indispensable elements, the reading, writing, and arithmetic, were neglected."[33]

And what specious inducements, asked Arnold, would the framers of the Code hold out in order to win the support of the country gentlemen and those members "with fair intentions but without special acquaintance with the subject, whose votes must decide the fate of the new scheme?" Why, such factitious enticements as these: "1. That the Code will repress the exorbitant pretensions of schoolmasters, and reduce the over-ambitious instruction of their highest classes; 2. *That it will carry*

31 Edward Baines, member for Leeds. See chap. 1, pp. 24–27, *supra*, for an example of his efforts on behalf of Voluntaryism and non-interference by the state in matters of education.

32 Super, II, pp. 214–15.

33 *Ibid.*, p. 215.

instruction into the 'waste places' of the country, and, in Dr. Vaughan's words, 'extend the advantages of education, to a certain though limited amount, to a larger number than heretofore.' "[34] And these promises, Arnold insisted, will prove "utterly and entirely delusive." The clear intention of these men is not a redistribution of the old resources, but a reduction by at least two-fifths of the present outlay. In such a bargain, no one wins; everybody loses.

In the letter of 19 February to his mother,[35] Arnold had mentioned Lowe's attack on the inspectors as quite relieving him from all scruples concerning his reply. Lowe had, in fact, made much of the alleged discrepancy between the reports of the inspectors and the report of the Newcastle Commission on the ineffectuality of instruction. Lowe had said on the floor of the Commons that "Had it been reported to us by the Inspectors, as it has been by the Commissioners, that in many schools three-fourths of the children were not instructed, we should have withdrawn the grant from those schools altogether."[36] His implication was that the inspectors had been derelict in their duty to the Department; that in order to perpetuate a system of lavish support, they had deliberately suppressed the true facts concerning the ineffectuality of instruction.

One would hardly expect Arnold to ignore such an attack upon the integrity of his reporting. His rejoinder comprised a great part of the third section of his reply – that is, the section dealing with the merit of the framers' design and "the prospect of its accomplishing what it intends." Arnold did not question the fact that but little learning was achieved under the present system; "the inspectors themselves declare it; the Royal Commissioners are careful to assure us that they assert this on the authority of the inspectors themselves, and not on that of their own Assistant-Commissioners." But of the conclusion that under present conditions marked improvement can be expected he was incredulous:

School-teachers deny it, school-managers deny it, Sir James Shuttleworth denies it, the most experienced of the inspectors deny it. They declare the fact of the ignorance in which so many poor children, after passing through our elementary schools, still remain; but they give an

34 *Ibid.,* p. 216. Apropos of the true authorship of this remark, see Super's correction (II, 354, note to 216: 35–7).
35 See p. 68, *supra.*
36 Hansard, Third Series, CLXV, 216.

explanation of this fact which is not that of the Royal Commissioners. "We know this," says Mr. Watkins, "*and we know also the cause*. It is the shortness of school-life. You cannot cram into the space of two or three years the instruction which ought to occupy five or six. Yet this is what is being done now, and must be done so long as the present inexorable demands of labour continue."[37]

The problem that Arnold confronted, and the popular attitudes toward it, are typical of all vast social undertakings: the inspectors – the professional men – had visited the schools and had, with proper expedience, adapted their judgments to the conditions prevalent there. The commissioners, appointed to study the real conditions and to report them accurately, had lacked the insights of the inspectors; but they had recognized the failure of the National system and had not hesitated to state the facts as these had appeared to them – and as the inspectors had indeed reported them. But the Philistine politicians, with their ingenuous zeal for economy, had seized upon an opportunity to reduce a none-too-cherished institution by the plausible expedient of paying only for tangible results. Their method was one of over-simplification, a device that put its victims, especially the inspectors, at a peculiar disadvantage in that they must assume the defensive while threatened with disaster, and knowing meanwhile that their own motives would appear to be selfish.

Arnold sought to resolve the dilemma by setting a clear definition of terms. What, he asked, is meant by *good reading*, and what ought the public reasonably to expect? The commissioners had said that under the prevailing conditions of school age and attendance, three-fifths of the scholars might be taught to read without conscious difficulty, whereas only one-fourth actually achieved that standard. But later, shifting their position slightly, they had adopted a special meaning for the phrase "to read without conscious difficulty," and had implied that it meant specifically, in one case, "*to read the Bible with intelligence*," and, in another, that the pupil be able "to *read the newspaper with sufficient ease to be a pleasure to himself and to convey information to listeners*." Now under these latter meanings, Arnold said, the contention of the commissioners that not more than one-fourth of the children in inspected schools learn to read *fairly* or *well* is undoubtedly correct; their implication that as

37 Super, II, 220–1. The Reverend Frederick Watkins was inspector of the Church of England schools in Yorkshire (Super, II, 355, note to 220: 34–221:1).

many as three-fifths should reach this standard is open to question. On the other hand, he continued,

If, when we speak of a scholar reading fairly or well, we merely mean that reading in his accustomed lesson-book, his provincial tone and accent being allowed for, his want of home-culture and refinement being allowed for, some inevitable interruptions in his school attendance being allowed for, he gets through his task fairly or well, then a much larger proportion of scholars in our inspected schools than the one-fourth assigned by the Royal Commissioners, may be said to read fairly or well. And this is what the inspectors mean when they return scholars as reading fairly or well.[38]

The real difficulty, of course, was cultural atrophy, always prevalent in the stultifying presence of poverty and social degradation. Shuttleworth had made much of this point in his "Letter to Earl Granville," effecting thereby a far more telling appeal to the general ear than Arnold appears to have comprehended. Shuttleworth spoke of the constant transiency of the wild nomadic hordes that thronged the manufacturing cities. Children enter a school, he said, who "have never lived but in a hovel; have never been in the street of a village or town; are unacquainted with the common usages of social life; perhaps, never saw a book; are bewildered by the rapid motion of crowds; confused in an assemblage of scholars. They have to be taught to stand upright, – to walk without a slouching gait, – to sit without crouching like a sheep dog," to practice some decency in the care of skin, hair, and dress. Such children "have no habits of attention, and are distracted by the Babel of sounds about them. The effort of abstraction required to connect a sound with a letter is at first impossible to them." Herded in among these dull and brutish oafs from the country are the sharp-witted, wild, restless Arabs of the street, accomplished, even as children, in the arts of thievery and beggary. "Such children have of late years been netted in shoals, – got into schools, – have been won, tamed, and, in some degree, taught."

Such, according to Shuttleworth, was the problem that the framers of the Revised Code would so confidently overcome. But, he protested,

is it not a mischievous fallacy to say that the work done is to be measured by the proficiency of such children in reading, writing, and arithmetic? All that has been done has been against wind and tide. At home –

38 *Ibid.*, p. 221.

misery, drunkenness, sullen despair, or the irritability of a dissolute life, drive the child into the street. Bad example at home lends its corruption to the foulness of the street of stews, and hiding holes. Are twenty scattered weeks, even if repeated in three successive years, enough to get rid of the wild, untamed barbarism of such children, and to graft on this civilisation that amount of knowledge of reading, writing, and arithmetic which the Commissioners say is so easy?[39]

Under such conditions, said Shuttleworth, the education of a people must require the labour of generations of teachers and learners. The first may gain little that may be measured; at best they will acquire an inclination, a favourable attitude toward the education of their own children. A truly adequate cultural leavening must come through slow accretion; and it is this that a wise and magnanimous government must patiently foster, waiting through many decades, perhaps, for the first fruits.

In their respective statements, it is Shuttleworth who makes the better popular appeal. But concerning the main problem – the enormous task of overcoming the cultural inertia of the nation – the two agree perfectly. According to Arnold, it had been the intelligent desire of the Newcastle commissioners to protect this larger cultural function of the schools; it had been this desire that had led them to recommend keeping "what we have called the *maintenance-grant* – the grant by which aid is given to a school not as a mere machine for teaching reading, writing, and arithmetic, but as a living whole with complex functions, religious, moral, and intellectual."[40] But the vice-president of the Committee of Council would now withdraw all support and encouragement from this broader, more civilizing function, and would reduce the whole basis of subsistence for the schools to "a system of prizes for three particular subjects."

And thus, "under specious pleas of simplifying," would the Revised Code assail the virtue of the old system. It would withdraw "all serious guidance, all initiatory direction by the State"; it would make the action of the state upon this "as mechanical, as little dynamical, as possible." It would turn the inspectors into a "set of registering clerks, with a mass of minute details to tabulate, such a mass as must, in Sir James Shuttleworth's words, 'necessarily withdraw their attention from the religious and general instruction, and from the moral features of the school." In fact the inspector will just hastily glance round the school, and then he

39 Kay-Shuttleworth, *Four Periods of Public Education*, pp. 583–5, note.
40 "The Twice-Revised Code" (Super, II, 224).

must fall to work at the 'log-books.' And this to ascertain the precise state of each individual scholar's reading, writing, and arithmetic."[41]

It is clear at this point that Arnold's indignation was mounting and that it might erupt at last in a direct castigation of his own superiors, the framers of the Code. Not the least of his provocations was the imminent plight of the inspectors under the proposed plan. The Revised Code, he said, would vastly increase the cost of inspection by superimposing a new group of county inspectors upon the old system. Arnold, on the other hand, would like to simplify and reduce. He would, in fact, decentralize the present system of inspection by relegating the more laborious function to local officials serving under the supervision of inspectors-general, the latter to be greatly diminished from the present number. He had seen such a system operating in Holland with signal success. The inspectors-in-chief would have large districts and be few in number. They would have what they are now denied because of their excessive number, "that access to their chief by which inspectors-general enlighten him as to what is really going on outside the walls of the central office." At present the inspectors are at once "very expensive, and a mob. Under the Revised Code they will be still more expensive, and still more a mob."[42]

Arnold touched but lightly in his article upon the prospects of the schoolmasters and of the training colleges under the Revised Code. And this is strange, for he had always been most solicitous for their welfare. It is true that he had felt a greater personal concern for the pupil-teacher system. In the report of 1861 to the Newcastle Commission, he had expressed a grave anxiety for the future of the pupil-teachers, as though he had already apprehended the impending danger:

Pupil-teachers – the sinews of English primary instruction, whose institution is the grand merit of our English State system, and its chief title to public respect; this, and, I will boldly say, the honesty with which that system has been administered. Pupil-teachers – the conception, for England, of the founder of English popular education, of the administrator whose conceptions have been as fruitful as his services were unworthily maligned, of Sir James Shuttleworth. In naming them, I pause to implore all friends of education to use their best efforts to preserve this institution to us unimpaired. ... Private liberality can repair the salaries of the schoolmasters, but no private liberality can

41 *Ibid.*, p. 235.
42 *Ibid.*, pp. 238–9.

create a body like the pupil-teachers. Neither can a few of them do the work of many. "Classes of twenty-five or thirty, and an efficient teacher to each class:" – that school-system is the best which inscribes these words on its banners.[43]

In this report, moreover, Arnold had expressed his personal reservations concerning the propriety of the augmentation grants – those premiums paid to teachers according to which of the three degrees of merit they had attained upon certification[44] – grants which the authors of the Revised Code now proposed to abolish. Knowing these facts, one is much less surprised to learn that in the *Fraser* article he is content not even to discuss "the much vexed question of the teachers' augmentation grants, by its handling of which the Revised Code has raised such a storm." He will not even claim that the teachers have "either a vested interest or a legal claim. They have only what is called, in common life, *a very hard case.*" But to reward them on the basis of their success in an examination for honours,[45] he feels, is a bad form of help for school-maintenance to take. In this matter, therefore, he will not engage to quarrel; and yet he deplores the way in which the principle of reduction has been managed. Surely, he said, this might have been accomplished by the Committee of Council "without wholly disregarding the hopes, the legitimate confidence, engendered by their own past operations; without throwing twenty thousand persons into despair."[46]

Concerning aid for the training colleges, he does not blame the Committee for wishing to set some reasonable limits. The state, he believes, has already blundered in aiding the creation of too many of these institutions,[47] "often in the wrong places, and at needless expense." But here again Arnold deplores the extreme, the inhumane method by which the limitation will be effected; he would have desired a consultative procedure, aiming at "processes which the training colleges might have

43 *The Popular Education of France* (Super, II, 114–15).

44 See pp. xix–xx, *supra*.

45 The certificates on which the three levels of the augmentation grants were based depended on the candidate's success in his final examinations, hence Arnold's implication that the grants were rewards for honours.

46 "The Twice-Revised Code" (Super, II, 239).

47 The state neither created nor established training colleges, but left this matter in the hands of the denominational organizations. The function of the state had been merely to issue grants in aid for buildings and to provide scholarships and other subsidies for students in attendance.

accepted, and which would not have abruptly deranged all their operations."[48]

It will be remembered that Arnold had proposed to discuss, at the close of his article, the recent changes announced by the vice-president, and "to examine the value and importance of these."[49] He did proceed to discuss them, but his consideration of the changes was thrown into shadow by the scintillating irony of his personal censure of that gentleman against whom his wrath had really been directed from the start:

But then throughout the whole speech of the real author of this Code –
Mr. Lowe – shines clearly forth the spirit which still animates him,
and which makes even his concessions valueless. That spirit is a spirit
of hostility to the system which he administers, and to its fundamental
principles. ... Reproached with inconsistency, he explains that he only
means to sweep away the *annual grants* of the present system. That is,
he means to sweep away just what is essential in the present system – its
maintenance grants, its recognition of the State's duty to aid schools
for the poor "in consideration of their discipline, efficiency, and general
character." And this he calls "not disturbing any fundamental principle
of the present system!" We suppose he must imagine that the "fundamental principle of the present system" is its vice-president, and that
so long as that functionary subsists, the system is whole ... he relieves
his mind by lamenting over the decay of that voluntary spirit which
once regarded all State-grants with such jealousy, by intimating that,
"were he at liberty to choose abstractly what he thought best for the
education of the country," he would have no grants at all. He has the
air of apologizing to the Voluntaries for not being able to give them
perfect satisfaction. We are convinced they will receive his apologies
most indulgently. His momentary bowing in the house of Rimmon
will be forgiven him. It is so evident that his heart is in the right place!
It is so manifest that his desires are in the heaven of Voluntaryism
with Mr. Baines, even though his practice be condemned to grope a
little longer in the earthly gloom of State-connexion!

But of his enmity to the present system, Mr. Lowe gave a yet more
striking proof than these apologies. It is understood that the inspectors
are, as a body, favourable to that system, and averse to the Revised
Code: their reports are quoted in contradiction of the assumptions on

48 "The Twice-Revised Code" (Super, II, 239-40).
49 See p. 69, *supra.*

which the Code is based. Mr. Lowe determined to punish them. The habits of English public life, the high tone of English public men, in general prescribe to a Minister the most punctilious consideration for those who serve under him. ... His generosity in this respect is one of Lord Palmerston's most popular qualities; rather than resist its impulse, he has incurred on more than one occasion serious embarrassment. From no such embarrassment will Mr. Lowe suffer. With the unscrupulousness of passion – growing desperate as the dangers of his "little subject" thickened round him – he, in his late speech, flung to the winds every restraint of official delicacy. In his Code he had sacrificed the principles of his department; in his speech he sacrificed its persons. The best part of that performance was an elaborate attack upon his own inspectors. Of this Lord Granville is incapable. But Lord Granville is not the real leader in this struggle.[50]

Thus does Arnold, an inspector, belabour the vice-president of his own department. One is inclined to ponder the ethics of a principle that enjoins the superior, but gives licence to the subordinate; most ethical restraints are interactive, binding the one reciprocally with the other. The vice-president had indeed attacked his own people publicly – that is, on the floor of the Commons. His remark was: "Had it been reported to us by the Inspectors, as it has been by the Commissioners ..."[51] He had clearly implied a deliberate negligence or deception in their reporting. His tone had been that of innuendo, with a taint, perhaps, of *grossièreté*.

But Arnold's statement has the ring of deliberate ironic ridicule. He seems, moreover, to be completely nonchalant in his manner. To his mother he wrote on 26 February:

At the end Lowe's speech is noticed sharply enough, but I have no fears whatever of Lowe's vengeance: first, because he cannot officially notice an article not signed with my name; secondly, because if he did, public opinion would support an inspector, attacked as we have been by Lowe, in replying in the only way open to us; thirdly, because, even if public opinion condemned what I did, it would never stand Lowe's resenting it, as he does precisely the same thing himself in the *Times*. Whenever he has a grudge at the Ministry of which he is a subordinate member he attacks it *there*. So I feel quite safe, and in

50 "The Twice-Revised Code" (Super, II, 241–2).
51 See p. 71, *supra*.

hopes of having done something to ward off the heaviest blow dealt at civilisation and social improvement in my time.[52]

For a month he maintained a cheerful mood. All of the letters from this point until 14 April contained allusions to the all-absorbing topic. On 5 March 1862, a letter to his mother was still confidently expansive. The sentiment of the country seemed to be shaping favourably; and a measure that was supposed to threaten the school-managers "ought to be very strong and sound in itself. And this the Revised Code is not, nor have its defenders ever made any really strong point, or got beyond being *plausible*." Arnold was sure that they could be beaten. With considerable pride he referred to his article:

I hope I have supplied a readable popular statement of the case against them which will take hold and do good. Lady de Rothschild[53] writes me word that she is making Disraeli read it, who wants just such a brief to speak from, and Shuttleworth and his Anti-Code Committee think it may be so useful that they have asked me to get leave from the editor for them to reprint it for distribution to members of Parliament. And, whether they get it from this article or not, I see Lord Derby and the Bishop of Oxford are coming to take the very ground I could wish them to take, namely, that the State has an interest in the primary school as a *civilising agent*, even prior to its interest in it as an *instructing agent*. When this is once clearly seen nothing can resist it, and it is fatal to the new Code. If we can get this clearly established in this discussion a great point will have been gained for the future dealings of the State with education, and I shall hope to see State-control reach in time our middle and upper schools.[54]

The consideration of Lowe's Minute of Council was resumed on the floor of the Commons on 25 March 1862, when the Right Honourable Spencer H. Walpole, member for Cambridge University,[55] rose to move

52 *Letters*, I, 159–60.
53 Arnold long maintained a warm friendship for Sir Anthony and Lady de Rothschild, frequently visiting them at Aston Clinton, their country estate.
54 *Letters*, I, 161–2 (February 26, 1861).
55 Spencer Walpole became Home Secretary in the Conservative Government of 1867, and was accordingly called upon to deal with the Hyde Park rioters in that year, the handling of which Arnold deplored in *Culture and Anarchy* (see pp. 132–4, *infra*).

"That this House will immediately resolve itself into a Committee to consider the best mode of distributing the Parliamentary Grants for Education now administered by the Privy Council; and, in Committee, to move the following Resolutions: ..."[56] The eleven resolutions centred the attention of the members upon specific faults in the Revised Code. The first alleged the inexpediency of basing the whole distribution of the grants for education upon an examination of each child in reading, writing, and arithmetic. The second exposed the fallacy of grouping the children by age rather than by classes for the purpose of the examination. The third pointed out the probable ineffectiveness of the Code in bringing education to the children of the poor in neglected districts. The fourth and fifth resolutions questioned the wisdom of withdrawing grants from pupils who had once passed the highest class and imposing the examination upon children under seven years of age. Others questioned the success of evening-schools when taught by masters who had already laboured all day in the day-schools, the unjust and impolitic treatment of the pupil-teachers, and the injustice of withdrawing grants from managers who had declined to advance the stipends and gratuities payable to the pupil-teachers. The last two resolutions, furthermore, were directed toward a circumvention in the future of such violent revisions of the educational structure as the authors of the Revised Code had undertaken, without a formal presentation of a printed schedule of specific clauses to be affected by the proposed changes, such schedule listing separately all articles to be cancelled or modified thereby – all action on such changes to be postponed until the printed schedule had lain upon the table of both Houses for at least one calendar month.[57]

Arnold had learned of Walpole's resolutions a fortnight earlier, for on 12 March 1862, he spoke of them in a letter addressed to his wife from Chelmsford:

I am delighted to find Walpole's Resolutions so good and firm as they are. I feared they would have been all shilly-shally. *These* Resolutions Lowe cannot possibly accept, or, if he does, he cannot possibly make the world believe that he is not giving up his Code by doing so. I am very much relieved, and the members of Parliament I see on circuit[58] are all full of the absurdity of "individual examinations." I have written

56 Hansard, Third Series, CLXVI, 21.
57 *Ibid.*
58 Arnold served as Marshall for his father-in-law, Sir William Wightman, one of the judges of the Court of Queen's Bench.

to Shuttleworth to tell him what I think of things. It is true the Bishop
of Oxford made a dreadful mistake by talking of his readiness to let
the Education grant reach £2,500,000;[59] that frightened the House of
Commons, which thinks the grant formidable already.[60]

On 24 March 1862, while still in court at Chelmsford, Arnold wrote to
his mother:

I have just heard from Shuttleworth that my paper is reprinted, and
that he has sent me twenty copies, and a copy to every member of each
House of Parliament.[61] I am extremely well pleased with Walpole's
Resolutions. The first affirms just the principle I want to have distinctly
affirmed – "To give rewards for proved good reading, writing, and
arithmetic is *not* the whole duty of the State towards popular education." It was reported by Lowe's friends that Lowe had information
of the purport of these Resolutions, and that he was not dissatisfied
with them, and I was afraid they would be very trimming and shilly-
shally, so I am the more pleased at finding them so firm and distinct.
Lowe cannot possibly accept them, or if he does, every one will see
that he confesses himself beaten by accepting them; and if he opposes
them, I think he will certainly be beaten. I see a great many members
of Parliament and country gentlemen on circuit. I find their impressions
of the offensiveness of the schoolmasters is strong, their impression that

59 On 4 March 1862, Samuel Wilberforce, the Bishop of Oxford, had expressed
   his belief, in an address before the House of Lords, "that less than three-fold
   of the present expense [namely, three times £803,000] would, on the largest
   possible estimate, cover the whole sum which, within a reasonable time, Parliament could under the old system be called upon to grant for the education
   of the people" (Hansard, Third Series, CLXV, 992). The speech was reported
   verbatim in the (London) *Times* of Wednesday, 5 March, on p. 6. It was
   Samuel Wilberforce who, at a scientific forum held at Oxford University in
   1860, alluded to Thomas Henry Huxley's simian ancestry and received Huxley's devastating counter-thrust (see Cyril Bibby, *T. H. Huxley, Scientist,
   Humanist, and Educator*, New York, 1960, pp. 68–70).
60 *Letters*, I, 163 (March 12, 1862).
61 The *Fraser* article was reprinted by Sir James Kay-Shuttleworth's Anti-Code
   Committee and distributed to all members of both Houses of Parliament.
   There is a copy of this reprint in the Rare Book Room at the University of
   Michigan General Library. It was bound into a volume, together with some
   twenty other items, by John Duke Coleridge. It is inscribed to Coleridge:
   "From the Author M. A." The collection was procured by Professor Super
   from Henry Danielson, a bookseller in Charing Cross Road.

too much is taught, and foolishly taught, in schools for the poor is strong; but their impression of the absurdity and probable expense of the individual examination is strongest of all. And it was this examination, on the basis of State-payments, that I have from the first attacked.[62]

The debate over Walpole's resolutions continued violently for two nights. But on the third day an amazing compromise was offered. As the order of business was resumed, Lowe arose to state that the Government had taken into consideration the debate which had occupied the House during the week, and that they had come to the conclusion that they ought, as far as was "consistent with their duty to the public purse and the public service, to meet the views so generally expressed by hon. Members of all parties in the course of the recent discussion."[63] He then offered the following concessions: 1. to agree that a substantial portion of the grant should be given on the general report of the inspector, namely, 4s. on the general attendance and 8s. on the results of the examinations; 2. to relinquish the plan to group the pupils by age for purposes of examination, and to leave the matter of grouping the children into six separate standards to the judgment of the masters; 3. to guarantee to the managers full restitution, even beyond the sum of the grant, for any outlay already expended upon pupil-teachers, but not withholding, in cases where the grants exceeded the outlay, any sums in excess of the declared expense; 4. "to accept the 10th and 11th Resolutions, which require all modifications or material alterations of the Code to be submitted to Parliament before they are carried into execution."[64]

Instantly the atmosphere of the Commons moderated. Walpole arose to congratulate the Committee "on the frank and generous manner in which the Government have endeavoured to obviate the objections which have been raised to certain portions of the Revised Code" and to suggest that the debate be terminated for an interval in order that "the House and the country should have a little time to consider whether they will accept the propositions." Disraeli[65] expressed his complete

62 *Letters*, I, 167.
63 Hansard, Third Series, CLXVI, 240.
64 *Ibid.*, 240–2.
65 Benjamin Disraeli, member for Buckinghamshire and Leader of the House during the third Derby Ministry (June 1866–February 1868). He succeeded Lord Derby as Prime Minister in February 1868.

satisfaction and gave "the Government credit for being actuated by the most honourable motives." William E. Forster[66] said that "he wished to express the very great pleasure with which he had heard the statement of the right hon. Gentleman the Vice-President of the Committee of Council, and also the hope it afforded him that the issue of the discussion in which the House had been engaged would be the real and permanent improvement of the system of popular education."[67]

Meanwhile, Arnold's own serenity had deteriorated. On 28 March 1862, the very date of Lowe's remarkable concessions, he wrote to his wife in a vein of grave apprehension:

I am puzzled to know how Greg[68] got my pamphlet. I never sent it him. I hope no one is sending it about in my name. I have no doubt the more it makes an impression the more incensed against me will the chiefs of the office become. I think perhaps the reason Lord Lansdowne does not answer my note[69] is that Lord Granville has spoken to him about the matter, and he is puzzled what to say to me. I don't think, however, they can eject me, though they can, and perhaps will, make my place uncomfortable. If thrown on the world I daresay we should be on our legs again before very long. Any way, I think I owed as much as this to a cause in which I have now a deep interest, and always shall have, even if I cease to serve it officially. ... I have a letter from Shuttleworth urgently begging me to answer Temple in the *Daily News*,[70] but I

66 William Edward Forster, Arnold's brother-in-law, was elected to Parliament on 11 February 1861 as member for Bradford (T. Wemyss Reid, *Life of the Right Honourable William Forster*, London, 1888, I, 330–1). Although a member of Lowe's Liberal party, Forster showed by his frank opposition to the Revised Code the staunch disinterestedness that characterized his public service. He became Chief Secretary for Ireland under the second Gladstone Government of 1880.

67 Hansard, Third Series, CLXVI, 242–8.

68 W. R. Greg, author of *The Enigmas of Life* [Russell's note]. The *Dictionary of National Biography* offers this comment: "It was Greg's especial function to discourage unreasonable expectations from political or even social reforms, to impress his readers with the infinite complexity of modern problems, and in general to caution democracy against the abuse of its power."

69 In a letter of 19 March to his mother, Arnold mentioned the note: "I am going to send a copy [of his pamphlet, the reprint of the *Fraser* article] with a note to Lord Lansdowne, and shall be very curious to see what he says to it" (*Letters*, I, 164).

70 Dr. Frederick Temple, headmaster of Rugby (1857–69); formerly Examiner in the Education Office and Inspector of Training Colleges (1848–57); and

think I have paid my contribution to the cause, considering what I risk by appearing for it, and I shall at any rate consider the matter well before I do anything more. What do you think?[71]

Two days later he had been to see William Forster and had regained his confidence through the reassuring counsel of that astute observer. His letter of 30 March to his wife is again confident and self-assured:

At half-past twelve Dick[72] and I started across the Park for Montagu Street,[73] getting there just as they were going to dinner. They were delighted to see us. William was there, and we had some most interesting talk about this compromise, which you will have been delighted with, but which still leaves a great deal to be done. That it is as good as it is, is in great measure due to William, his earnestness, his thorough knowledge of the subject, and the courage which his reputation for honesty gave to other Liberals to follow him in opposing the Code. I shall now get off the task of answering Temple. I find William thinks my letter in answer to Lord Overstone one of the most telling and useful strokes in the whole contest. William, however, is of opinion they cannot touch me, and would bring a storm on their heads if they did.[74]

Arnold's "letter in answer to Lord Overstone" was another anonymous attempt to oppose the supporters of the Code. The letter, entitled "Principle of Examination," appeared in the *Daily News* on 25 March 1862, the very day that Walpole presented his resolutions in the Lower House.[75] It bore the subscription, "A Lover of Light." Five days earlier, in a speech before the House of Lords, Lord Overstone[76] had expressed

---

later Archbishop of Canterbury (1896–1902). His letter upholding the principles of the Revised Code appeared in the (London) *Times* of Tuesday, 25 March 1862, p. 5.

71 *Letters*, I, 168.

72 His third son, Richard Penrose Arnold, born 14 November 1855.

73 During William's second parliamentary session, the Forsters lived at No. 18 Montagu Street (Reid, I, 346).

74 *Letters*, I, 168–9.

75 "The Principle of Examination" may be found in Super, II, 244–6, and in Fraser Neiman, *Essays, Letters, and Reviews by Matthew Arnold* (Cambridge, Mass., 1960), pp. 36–8. See also William Fraser Connell, *The Educational Thought and Influence of Matthew Arnold* (London, 1950), p. 216.

76 Samuel Jones Loyd, eminent banker and former member of Parliament for Hythe. He was raised to the peerage on 5 March 1860 as Baron Overstone (*Dictionary of National Biography*).

his complete confidence in the practice of examinations, both as a test of educational integrity on the part of the school, and as a stimulus to the pupils' exertion.[77] Citing his own early experience as a student under Charles James Blomfield,[78] he averred that "The people of this country might rest assured that where a school submitted willingly to the test of examination the system of instruction followed there was a sound one; and, on the other hand, they might with certainty come to an opposite conclusion wherever they found an unwillingness or an inability to undergo such a test."

Arnold's reply is based upon his opponent's personal example; his question is –

Is it a good thing to make the scholar's success in his examination the sole measure of the payment of those who educate him? If Lord Overstone's father had proposed to Bishop Blomfield to make his son's performance in an examination at the end of the year the basis for fixing what he should pay for that year's schooling, and proposed this before the Bishop could know the admirable talents which Lord Overstone, under his care, was to develop, would the excellent tutor have "willingly submitted"? If he did not submit, ought he to have submitted? Would his "shrinking" from this test have implied that there was "something unsound" even in that tuition which has made Lord Overstone what we see him? Would the Bishop have deserved all the depreciatory sarcasm of Mr. Lowe, all the exquisite amenities of the *Times*, for shrinking from it?[79]

On 14 April in a letter to his mother, Arnold again expressed a reviving confidence. By this time he had resolved to fight for a larger proportion – namely, one-half – for the maintenance grant; as for that portion which represented the state's real debt to elementary education, he would not accept, he said, a secondary character; "it must be at least equal to the other."[80]

I believe Shuttleworth and his constituents would thoroughly endorse these views, and that the whole Tory party will go for the half grant

---

77 Hansard, Third Series, CLXV, 1868–9.
78 Charles James Blomfield, Rector of St. Botolph, Bishopsgate, and Bishop of London from 1828 to 1856.
79 "The Principle of Examination" (Super, II, 244–5; Neiman, 37–8).
80 See Lowe's concession no. 1 on p. 82, *supra*.

(carrying their doctrinaires, like Stafford Northcote, along with them) ; the sound Liberals like Wm. Forster will join them, the Government will be beaten, the Code will be dropped, and Lowe will go out. This, at least, is what I now hope for. He has declared that he has been humiliated enough, and that he will not accept any further interference with his Code, but give it up and go out, "and others," he says, "will go with me." Whether this means Lingen or Lord Granville, or both, I don't know. But I remain as still as a mouse to see how things turn.[81]

Lowe's resignation was to be delayed for two full years. It came about, it is true, over an issue that still echoed the old rancours generated by the conflict over the Revised Code. He was accused on the floor of the Commons by Lord Robert Cecil of mutilating the reports of the inspectors; and despite Lowe's forthright denials, a resolution was passed: "That, in the opinion of this House, the mutilation of the Reports of Her Majesty's Inspectors of Schools, and the exclusion from them of statements and opinions adverse to the educational views entertained by the Committee of Council, while matter favourable to them is admitted, are violations of the understanding under which the appointment of the Inspectors was originally sanctioned by Parliament, and tend to destroy the value of their Reports."[82] This action was taken on 12 April 1864, and six days later Lowe announced his resignation.

He did not remain undefended, however. A month later, on 12 May, a motion was passed "that a Select Committee be appointed to inquire into the practice of the Committee of Council on Education with respect to the Reports of Her Majesty's Inspectors of Schools."[83] The select committee reported on 26 July 1864 and moved a resolution completely exonerating the former vice-president and rescinding the action which had censured and condemned him.[84]

Meanwhile, the popular controversy over the Revised Code continued unabated in the columns of the press. Although Arnold had, as he said, paid his contribution to the cause, "considering what I risk by appearing for it," he could not refrain from joining in the popular debate. He did not answer Temple,[85] as he had earlier resolved, because Lowe's compromise over the Walpole Resolutions had made such an effort quite

81 *Letters*, I, pp. 170–1.
82 Hansard, Third Series, CLXXIV, 897–914.
83 *Ibid.*, CLXXV, 398.
84 *Ibid.*, CLXXVI, 2067–81.
85 See note 70, *supra*; also Super, II, 377–8, note to 301: 26–28.

unnecessary. He did, however, write two more attacks on the Code, which his friend Cumin published in the weekly *London Review*. The first, entitled "The Code out of Danger," appeared on 10 May 1862; the second, entitled "Mr. Walter and the Schoolmasters' Certificates," came a year later.[86] Both exemplify his telling irony and press forward his anonymous denunciation of Robert Lowe. The first reads like the celebration of a great victory – a Pyrrhic one obviously, for it assumes the full totality of the vice-president's humiliating defeat on the compromise of 28 March. Likening his adversary to a great retriever dog, Arnold now maintains that "The fight was warm, but it is over; and Mr. Lowe has swum to shore with two principles in his mouth. The Opposition having forced him to abandon a great deal else, are content to see him land with these two principles, shake himself, and set about putting them in operation."[87]

The two principles Lowe had salvaged were: (1) "to know no one financially but the manager of the school," and (2) "to have some individual examination of the scholars." But these two principles, Arnold now contends, had never been opposed by Lowe's adversaries, who had merely deplored his making the individual examinations the *sole* basis of payments. "To this objection they have compelled Mr. Lowe to yield. All their success is here."

In the light of the future drudgery compounded for an inspector henceforth required to maintain the letter of the Code, the claim of success seems quite extravagant. Two-thirds of the grant must now be paid on the results of the examination, and one-third on attendance. The labour entailed upon the inspectors would be as great in any event as though the whole grant were to be based upon the results of the examination.

But now Arnold would hold it otherwise. "To have succeeded here," he said, "is much. A principle far more real and important than either of Mr. Lowe's two principles has been saved. In direct contradiction to Mr. Lowe it has been successfully maintained, that to give rewards for proved good reading, writing, and arithmetic is *not* the whole duty of the State towards popular education."[88]

The enemies of popular education, however, had sensed a victory, and were prepared to go much farther in their attacks upon a hated system

86 These two anonymous articles were first traced by Professor Super from clues found in Arnold's quarterly accounts (see vol. II, "Editor's Preface," p. v).

87 Super, II, 247.

88 *Ibid.*, p. 248.

than the limitations of the Revised Code would have permitted – farther even than the vice-president of the Council was prepared to follow. The member for Berkshire, the Honourable John Walter,[89] saw in the new Code an opportunity to bring another aspect of education, the certification of teachers, under its beneficent control. If payments for instruction were to be based truly upon the principle of results, he reasoned, why then should the credentials of teachers require any further notice? Accordingly, on 5 May 1862, with the Commons convened in committee, Walter moved the following resolution: "That to require the employment of Certificated Masters and Pupil Teachers by Managers of Schools, as an indispensable condition of their participation in the Parliamentary Grants, is inexpedient and inconsistent with the principle of payment for results which forms the basis of the Revised Code."[90]

Ostensibly Walter's motion was intended to relieve those schools not employing certificated masters from the automatic disqualification for receiving grants. His plan would permit the dispensing of aid impartially to all schools according to one simple standard – the measured results of their instruction. Walter came armed with the vice-president's own words to support him. Lowe had said: "If we were logical and consistent, which I admit we are not, we should lay down no rules as to the sort of teachers that should be employed in schools. We should leave it to the managers to select such machinery as they thought proper; and if the children passed the examination, that would be enough for us."[91] Lowe had, however, gone on to say explicitly that his remark was not intended to repudiate the principle of certification; he had insisted, in fact, on the same right to require a properly educated teacher as then prevailed in the requirements for entry into the legal or the medical professions.

But Walter rejected the apt analogy with law and medicine, because in the case of doctors and lawyers, he said, payment might quite properly be demanded without reference to results. "But if you threw open the legal or medical profession, and established the principle of 'no cure no pay,' as you profess to do now with regard to schools, I do not see what right you would have to require degrees or any other test of profi-

---

89 Walter succeeded his father as chief proprietor of the (London) *Times*. As member for Nottingham, and later for Berkshire, he was elected as a Liberal-Conservative, but he really belonged to the extreme right wing of the Liberal party (*Dictionary of National Biography*).

90 Hansard, Third Series, CLXVI, 1257–8.

91 *Ibid.*, 1247–8.

ciency. ... Therefore I think that the right hon. Gentleman's [Lowe's] argument breaks down."[92]

"Claptraps," said Arnold, in his article on the subject, "are like young chickens, they always come home to roost."[93] And certainly they had now come home, a whole devil's brood of them. So grave was the threat to the Council's position, that the vice-president felt compelled to intervene. His speech before the House of Commons was a masterpiece of analysis and explication. First of all, he was forced to admit, as Arnold had contended, that "payment by results," as the Committee of Council had envisioned the principle, no longer prevailed within the current operation of the Revised Code: "What I want to point out to the Committee is that payment by results exists no longer in the present Code, and that the proposition we have before us [doing away with certification] really does away with the former security we had by appropriations to certificated masters, who had been carefully trained and taught for the purpose, and substitutes for it an imperfect security by examination."[94]

But the greatest menace in Walter's resolution, Lowe clearly saw, lay in another direction – in the vast extension of government payments to schools now disqualified from receiving such aid because they employed no certificated master: "You are asked to admit, as far as I can form an estimate, some 654,000 children more to the capitation grant, and to introduce between 15,000 and 16,000 fresh schools. What demands may in consequence be made on the Exchequer it is at present impossible to calculate. They would, no doubt, be very considerable, nor could we hope for any large diminution of the grant until the existing race of pupil-teachers had passed away.[95]

Lowe saw also another apparition in Walter's motion, the probable destruction of the training colleges, an aim the Committee of Council had never had in mind.

I am not now speaking of whether it is advisable to keep up those colleges or not, but I cannot conceive that they can be ultimately supported unless you hold out some object to those by whom they are passed. If you had established an examination of the stringent character

92 *Ibid.*, 1248.
93 "Mr. Walter and the Schoolmasters' Certificates" (Super, II, 257).
94 Hansard, Third Series, CLXVI, 1268.
95 *Ibid.*, 1268–9.

which was originally proposed, it might be that the superior training required to fit pupils for the examination might make it worth a man's while to go to a training college; but now that you have determined to adopt a more lax system, it is doubtful whether this would be the case to such an extent as to secure the maintenance of those colleges.[96]

Finally, Lowe called attention to an inaccuracy in the text of the resolution: "to require the employment of certificated masters and pupil-teachers by managers of schools as an indispensable condition of their participation in the Parliamentary grant is inexpedient." It was not the present practice, Lowe explained, to require the employment of pupil-teachers, "and the Resolution cannot, therefore, be very well put in its present shape." He suggested that the words "and pupil-teachers" should be omitted.

Walter immediately complied by offering an amended motion. Thereupon, the question was put, and the Committee divided: Ayes, 156; Noes, 163; Majority to defeat, 7.[97]

It is fully evident that the offering of Walter's resolution, and the fanatical character of the debate thereon, had occasioned considerable embarrassment for Robert Lowe, and that Arnold employed his advantage with cogent analysis and telling rejoinder. The certificate of merit, he observed, is a document "attesting that the holder has passed a satisfactory examination in the subjects of elementary instruction." As such, it is demanded of the candidate in every country of Europe. But it appears that Mr. Walter, the member for Berkshire, has in his privately supported school at Bearwood a master "without this appendage." Therefore, "let us have free trade in education. *Sursum corda.* Down with tails!"[98] Waiving for the moment the absurdity of Walter's proposal, Arnold turned immediately to an exposition of the predicament in which the state and Robert Lowe now found themselves. First of all, the state could not possibly accomplish the examination of the results of instruction that the revolutionary proposal demanded. In addition to the increased burden to be borne by the inspectors of the schools aided formerly by the parliamentary grants, the state must henceforth extend its "inquisition" into every school in England (some 15,000 more schools, Lowe had estimated, with a population of some 654,000 more children). Inspection on such an extended scale would disintegrate into a "mere

96 *Ibid.*, 1269–70.
97 *Ibid.*, 1270–1.
98 Super, II, 257–8.

farce," or it would "prove so ruinously expensive" that it could not be continued for six months. But, Arnold continued:

Mr. Walter is fortunate. ... He has to deal with a Minister who has himself used all Mr. Walter's clap-traps, and who now finds them turned against himself. *Let us have free trade in education,* is a cry of which Mr. Lowe is the original proprietor. Last year he and the *Times* thought they could not let us hear it too often. Last year Mr. Lowe was never weary of disparaging all securities except this one security of results; he could not sufficiently scout the notion of paying for "means," instead of solely paying for "results;" he had no words strong enough to express his scorn for the hollowness of the old system of the Privy Council Office. He rated tails very cheap then. If he defends them now, it is not because he believes in them a bit more than Mr. Walter does, but because Mr. Walter's crusade against them threatens him with a personal embarrassment.[99]

Certainly Lowe's embarrassment was real, and most certainly Arnold relished his discomfiture. He closes with Molière's hilarious riposte on *Le Mari confondu*: "*Tu l'as voulu, Georges Dandin, tu l'as voulu!*"

THE EFFECTS OF THE REVISED CODE

Admirers of Arnold should exercise some caution in imputing ulterior motives to the vice-president. Arnold's solicitude for the broader, more cultural aspects of the educational programme was certainly justified, but there were undoubtedly some factors in the controversy which he failed to discern clearly. One of these factors was the mounting apprehension of Robert Lowe, and of the Liberal leaders in general, over the rapidly augmenting scope of the education system, with its centralized department of state, entirely in the hands of the politicians in power. For a government, its immense personnel represented a bureaucratic patronage of commanding scope. For his strenuous efforts toward decentralization of the control of British schools, Robert Lowe receives the approbation of one historian at least: "Perhaps Robert Lowe, in apparently doing a grave injustice to a whole generation, in reality by this early measure of decentralisation saved English education once and for all from the pitfalls which have ensnared the systems of so many other

99 *Ibid.,* 258-9.

countries; notably Germany, Italy, and to a less extent, France."[100] And still another said of him: "The authors of the attack, however, had the personal gratification of driving from office the most able Minister who has yet held the post of Vice-President; who, if he initiated no large measure for the establishment of education on a broad and liberal basis, brought the system which existed to a practical test of usefulness, and converted a pretentious, but delusive plan, into an actual educational experiment."[101] Granting the possible wisdom of these motives, one must reflect on how contrary they were to Arnold's most cherished theory of education and of government; to his faith in an expanded electorate, enlightened through the beneficent power of sweetness and light; to his concept of the state as the embodiment of "our best self," a doctrine which he had already clearly enunciated, and which he was later to proclaim as the cardinal principle of *Culture and Anarchy*.

Certainly the results of the Revised Code were neither an improvement of instruction nor a simplification of the inspector's role. The dividing of the grant between *maintenance* and *examination* meant an actual doubling of the burden of accounting. In his "General Report for the Year 1863," Arnold commented chiefly on two effects of the Revised Code: (1) the effect upon the function of the inspector, and (2) the effect upon the general culture of the school, both adverse.[102] Concerning the first, Arnold deplored the passing away of the old objective of the inspector's visit, "promoting the intellectual force of schools." Under the old system, one had conversed with the pupils class by class, calling out individuals at random to demonstrate their powers of reading, and freely questioning the class on the subjects they had studied. As one progressed into the upper levels, he discovered more and more centres of interest, such as English grammar, geography, and history, with a special entry on his report form calling for the inspector's comments on the general cultural achievement in each subject. There had been variety and interest in the activity for the inspector, and for the pupils and the teacher as well. The power of the pupils in composition had been tested, together with the teacher's method of handling the subject; and con-

100 G. A. N. Lowndes, *The Silent Social Revolution* (London, 1937), p. 11.
101 Adams, p. 189.
102 Edmund Mackenzie Sneyd-Kynnersley, one of Arnold's younger fellow-inspectors, said of him that "He did what we were strictly forbidden to do, and what we lesser lights were afraid to do; he freely criticised the Code, and freely suggested improvements. And throughout there ran the three threads of humour, irony, and hard common sense" (*H. M. I., Some Passages in the Life of One of H. M. Inspectors of Schools*, London, 1908, pp. 197–8).

structive criticism had been offered then and there, both to the pupils and to the teacher. The result had been a stimulating appraisal and taking of stock, the school receiving advice and direction, and the inspector obtaining a fairly reliable estimate of the cultural life of the school.

And now, under the new system, the function of the inspector had degenerated into a complex regimen of meticulous recording of details. Arnold was disposed to complain bitterly of this dull and worrisome drudgery:

Few can know till they have tried what a business it is to enter in a close-ruled schedule, as an examination goes on, three marks for three different things against the names of 200 children whom one does not know one from the other, without putting the wrong child's mark in the wrong place. Few can know how much delay and fatigue is unavoidably caused before one can get one's 600 communications fairly accomplished, by difficulty of access to children's places, difficulty in seeing clearly in the obscurer parts of the school-room, difficulty of getting children to speak out – sometimes of getting them to speak at all – difficulty of resisting, without feeling oneself inhuman, the appealing looks of master or scholars for a more prolonged trial of a doubtful scholar.[103]

Then there were inquiries to be made into the details of administration: the log-book, the portfolio, the accounts, pupil-teacher contracts and stipends; and even the station in life of the pupils' parents, to discover whether or not they were entitled to the assistance of the state. For the recording of such data, the inspector had found it necessary to sacrifice the best portion of his former influence, the stimulation of the intellectual vigour and cultural life of the school. For a man of Arnold's temperament, this must have been a truly enervating circumstance.

The second adverse effect was the exaggerated attention drawn to the rudimentary subjects, with a reciprocal neglect of the broader, more cultural fields upon which a liberal education must really depend. If the teachers and managers must look for two-thirds of their income from the grants based upon the results in reading, writing, and arithmetic, naturally they would be inclined to expend their greatest effort upon teaching these things. Again, in the reports for 1865 and for 1869, Arnold lamented the passing of the old cultural ideal. In the report for the latter

103 *Reports on Elementary Schools*, pp. 102–3.

year, he discovered even the prevalence of evasive practices among teachers, who were more anxious to protect their shrinking incomes than scrupulous over the quality of their instruction:

I have repeatedly said that it seems to me the great fault of the Revised Code, and of the famous plan of *payment by results*, that it fosters teaching by rote; I am of that opinion still. I think the great task for friends of education is, not to praise *payment by results*, which is just the sort of notion to catch of itself popular favour, but to devise remedies for the evils which are found to follow the application of this popular notion. The school examinations in view of *payment by results* are, as I have said, a game of mechanical contrivance in which the teachers will and must more and more learn how to beat us. It is found possible, by ingenius preparation, to get children through the Revised Code examination in reading, writing, and ciphering, without their really knowing how to read, write, and cipher.[104]

Quite in accord with the prediction of Sir James Kay-Shuttleworth that the Revised Code would result in a severe reduction in state support for schools, the amounts of the annual grants immediately and steadily declined. From the £836,920 of 1859, the total grant fell to £693,078 in 1865, and to £511,324 in 1869. Such a loss to the schools directly affected all teachers, pupil-teachers, and school officials who had been dependent for their living upon a substantial addition from the state to the tenuous trickle of school pence and local charities. At the same time, this radical decrease in the funds for the support of schools was accompanied by a considerable increase in the number of pupils attending, an increase which resulted from a general upward trend in the popularity of education, rather than from any stimulus occasioned by the Code itself. The effect of the diminishing revenues under such conditions of increased labour was the inevitable demoralization of the teaching profession. In Arnold's "General Report for the Year 1867," he devoted his attention chiefly to this third adverse effect of the Revised Code.

At the time of writing this report, Arnold had just returned from his second visit to the Continent under the auspices of the Taunton, or Schools Inquiry, Commission of 1865. Thus he was able to make two comparisons: (1) the contrast between his present impressions of the English schools and those of his former return in 1859; and (2) the

104 *Ibid.*, 136.

differences in the quality of the English schools from those on the Continent. Both were unfavourable:

I cannot say that the impression made upon me by the English schools at this second return to them has been a hopeful one. I find in them, in general, if I compare them with their former selves, a deadness, a slackness, and a discouragement which are not the signs and accompaniments of progress. If I compare them with the schools of the Continent I find in them a lack of intelligent life much more striking now than it was when I returned from the Continent in 1859.

This change is certainly to be attributed to the school legislation of 1862. That legislation has reduced the rate of public expenditure upon schools, has introduced the mode of aid which is commonly called *payment by results*, and has withdrawn from teachers all character of salaried public servants. ... in my report to the Royal Commission of 1859 I said, after seeing the foreign schools, that our pupil-teachers were, in my opinion, "the sinews of English public instruction;" and such in my opinion they, with the ardent and animated body of schoolmasters who taught and trained them, undoubtedly were. These pupil-teachers and that body of schoolmasters were called into existence by the school legislation of 1846;[105] the school legislation of 1862 struck the heaviest possible blow at them; and the present slack and languid condition of our elementary schools is the inevitable consequence.[106]

In support of his contention, Arnold offered some startling statistical data: in 1861 the proportion of pupil-teachers to pupils was one to thirty-six; in 1866 it had decreased to one to fifty-four. The decline of the profession was reflected in the attendance at the training colleges; in 1862, no less than 2,513 candidates had presented themselves; in 1866, the number had shrunk to 1,478. And yet the number of schools depending upon this source for their recruitment of teachers had increased over the same interval from 6,258 to 8,303; while the population of these schools had increased from 919,935 in 1862 to 1,082,055 in 1866.[107]

105 Arnold applies the term *legislation* to what was technically not legislation at all. Both the Minutes of 1846 and the Minute of 1862 were, properly speaking, executive orders, although the debates on the floor of the Commons had led, in the latter case, to considerable amendment.
106 *Reports on Elementary Schools*, pp. 110–11.
107 *Ibid.*, p. 111.

The performance of the pupil-teachers, moreover, Arnold believed, had become weaker and more inaccurate. In assigning the reason for this loss of professional power, he pointed to the insecurity of tenure under which the candidate must now aspire, and also to the limited instruction he now received from the master. Formerly, the pupil-teacher was protected by an indenture "which he was accustomed to regard as absolutely binding him for five years"; now his contract was terminable by notice or by payment. Then, he was allowed seven and a half hours of instruction per week from the principal teacher at intervals taken out of the regular school day when he could enjoy the undivided attention of the master; now, he might have only five hours, and these might be given in the night-school, where the principal-teacher's attention must be shared with the whole school, and where his energy might be dissipated by a long day's labour. But looming above all these disadvantages, there was the lost enthusiasm of the old master "who ten years ago was rewarded for teaching him, was proud of his own profession, was hopeful, and tried to communicate his pride and hope to his apprentice."[108]

The deep nostalgic note in the reports for these years reflects the sympathy and fellow-feeling that Arnold had come to share with the teachers of the schools which he inspected. It would be awkward to impugn, were one so inclined, so generous, so magnanimous an emotion. It may be often politic to ignore the victims of those who blunder in high places, and to be discreetly silent where one's superiors are disposed to temporize, but Arnold disdained prudence under such restraints. The stubborn strength of his fidelity to the teachers is shown in a letter of 9 July 1866, written to the Honourable Mr. H. A. Bruce, the vice-president of the Committee of Council who succeeded Robert Lowe:

West Humble.
Dorking.

I bore you with the enclosed, about which I was speaking to you the other day, in order that you may see for yourself what is that ulceration of spirit I described to you as existing among many, I believe most, of the better schoolmasters formed under the old system. Their merits were great, and they have a strong feeling that their merits were not the least recognised and that they were treated with harshness and contempt. Perhaps you might be able to find opportunity for a kind expression about them; it would come well from you who are, after all,

108 *Ibid.*, pp. 111-13.

quite unfettered by your past as to the Revised Code;[109] and I am sure it is indispensable for any future operation of importance, that something more of attachment and confidence towards the Committee of Council should be awakened among the body of educationists than exists at present.

I have answered Mr. Hardy's letter so it may burn when you have read it – and this note of mine requires no answer.

In spite of the Times I must say that I am very glad it is Mr. Corry rather than Mr. Adderley[110] who is to succeed you – but for your going I am heartily sorry, Believe me

Ever very truly yours,
Matthew Arnold. – [111]

The system of "payment by results" continued in force until 1900, twelve years after Arnold's death, when a new Code provided for the granting of government aid in one block, at a fixed rate per pupil, subject only to the inspector's favourable comment upon the general efficiency of the school.[112] While the effects of the system may have been fully as vicious as Arnold felt them to be, it would be an over-simplification to attribute the blunder entirely to the political cupidity of Robert Lowe, or to impugn Lowe's intelligence. Looking back upon the incident through the mellowing light of his last years, Arnold himself spoke of the former vice-president as "an acute and brilliant man to whom pretentiousness with unsoundness was very distasteful and contemptible."[113] But reflecting now dispassionately on the circumstances of that tempestuous time, he still maintained the premises of his former position:

The improved schools had been but a dozen years at work; they had had to civilise the children as well as to instruct them; reading, writing, and ciphering were not the whole of education; people who were so

109 Henry Austin Bruce (Lord Aberdare) had been Undersecretary of State for the Home Department in 1862. He served as vice-president of the Committee of Council from 1864 to 1866, and was succeeded by Henry Thomas L. Corry.

110 Charles Bowyer Adderley (Lord Norton) had preceded Robert Lowe as vice-president in 1858.

111 From the collection of Professor Carlton F. Wells, of the University of Michigan.

112 Binns, p. 232.

113 Matthew Arnold, "Schools," in Thomas Humphry Ward, ed., The Reign of Queen Victoria, 2 vols. (London, 1887), II, 258.

impatient because so many of the children failed to read, write, and cipher correctly did not know what the children were when they came to school, or what were the conditions of the problem which their educators had to solve ...

... I have always thought that the Commissioners [of the Newcastle Commission], finding in the state of the junior classes and of the elementary matters of instruction a point easy to be made and strikingly effective, naturally made it with some excess of energy and pressed it too hard. I knew the English schools well in this period between 1850 and 1860, and at the end of it I was enabled to compare them with schools abroad. Some preventable neglect of the junior classes, some preventable shortcoming in the elementary instruction, there was; but not nearly so much as was imagined. What there was would have been sufficiently met by a capitation grant on individual examination, not for the whole school, but for the children between seven or eight years old and nine or ten, a grant which would then have been subsidiary, not principal. General "payment by results" has been a remedy worse than the disease which it was meant to cure.[114]

A year earlier (7 April 1886) Arnold had given substantially the same testimony before the Cross Commission.[115] And thus with the old firm convictions he ponders serenely, if a little sadly, the issues of his most intense, his most energetic political intervention. In the struggle he had met defeat at the hands of the intrenched forces of Philistinism – a defeat that would not only retard the progress of British education for a whole generation, but would entail for him personally a dull and picayune labour throughout the remaining twenty-three years of his inspectorship. What a laboratory example it must have been for Arnold, moving at that very time toward a statement of his definitive theory of social reform in *Culture and Anarchy*!

114 *Ibid.*, pp. 259–60.
115 *First Report of the Royal Commissioners Appointed to Inquire into the Working of the Elementary Education Acts, England and Wales* (London, 1886), Answers 5810–26.

IV

Arnold's Vision of A Cultural Reformation

SECONDARY EDUCATION FOR THE MIDDLE CLASS

Before Arnold wrote *Culture and Anarchy,* he had been sent, as has been mentioned, upon a second mission to the Continent (from April to November 1865), where as an assistant commissioner for the Schools Inquiry Commission he studied the secondary schools and universities of France, Italy, Germany, and Switzerland. Returning from this second tour in the late autumn of 1865, he was reminded of the advice he had given on his return from his first commission abroad in 1859. *"Organise your secondary instruction,"* he had said in his report to the Newcastle Commission. And now, reflecting over the six-year interval, he observed a little ruefully that the advice had gone completely unheeded: "the hubbub of our sterile politics continued, ideas of social reconstruction had not a thought given them, our secondary instruction is still the chaos it was." And yet, strengthened and confirmed in his former convictions, he concluded the second report with the same injunction: *"Organise your secondary and your superior instruction."*[1]

It was in Germany that he had found the finest example of his humanistic ideal of education. The more one observed the German schools, he had discovered, the more one was impressed with the power of humane studies. Here one witnessed a genuine love of study – a pursuit of the humanities and of science for their own sakes. In Germany, he believed, a predisposition toward the things of the mind had been carefully nurtured, both by the content of the studies offered, and by the reasonable method of instruction. Arnold never ceased to admire this humanizing aspect of German education. Late in his active life, as he made his last

1 *Schools and Universities on the Continent* (Super, IV, 328).

report on the elementary schools of Germany (1886), he was drawn to
comment once more on this enviable result:

Again and again I find written in my notes, *The children human*. They
had been brought under teaching of a quality to touch and interest them,
and were being formed by it. The fault of the teaching in our popular
schools at home is, as I have often said, that it is so little formative; it
gives the children the power to read the newspaper, to write a letter, to
cast accounts, and gives them a certain number of pieces of knowledge,
but it does little to touch their nature for good and to mould them. ... The
excellent maxim of that true friend of education, the German schoolmaster, John Comenius, "The true aim is to train generally all who are
born men to all which is human," does to some considerable degree govern the proceedings of popular schools in German countries, and now in
France also, but in England hardly at all.[2]

Temperamentally, Arnold favoured the kind and generous teacher.
Rigorism, in its stern, ascetic sense, was foreign to his nature. He had a
strong antipathy for the disciplinary motive in examinations, and he
thought that English boys were crammed and examined to the point of
surfeiture and dullness. Speaking of the French *lycées*, he said that they
were "guiltless of one preposterous violation of the laws of life and health
committed by our own schools," the competitive examination for places
on their foundations. It was in Prussia, again, that he saw the wise observance of the golden mean in these matters: examinations drawn up so
as "to tempt candidates to no special preparation and effort, but to be
such as 'a scholar of fair ability and proper diligence, may at the end of
his school course come to with a quiet mind and without a painful preparatory effort tending to relaxation and torpor as soon as the effort is
over.' " Arnold elucidated this point with special care, as though cognizant of the danger involved in assailing a popular fetish:

The total cultivation (*Gesammtbildung*) of the candidate is the great
matter, and this is why the two years of *prima* are prescribed, "that the
instruction in this highest class may not degenerate into a preparation for
the examination, that the pupil may have the requisite time to come
steadily and without overhurrying to the fulness of the measure of his
powers and character, that he may be securely and thoroughly formed,

2 *Special Report on Certain Points Connected with Elementary Education in
Germany, Switzerland, and France* (London, 1886), p. 14.

instead of being bewildered and oppressed by a mass of information hastily heaped together." All *tumultuarische Vorbereitung* and all stimulation of vanity and emulation is to be discouraged, and the examination, like the school, is to regard *das Wesentliche und Dauernde* – the substantial and enduring.[3]

In the German universities also, Arnold thought that he had discovered a true spiritual disposition toward the things of the mind. In Austria, on the other hand, "a country which believes in the things of the mind as little as we do," the examinations were applied with a "mechanical faith" much like that of the English. And for this a country pays with a lowered intellectual life. "All I say is," he concluded, "that a love for things of the mind is what we want, and that examinations will never give it."[4]

Emanating from these practical comments, one may discern an aura of regret – a sad, enduring awareness that in England the humanizing power of letters was so little understood. The stultifying abuses of cram and quiz were such as to preclude all access to the *Alterthumswissenschaft* of the German schools. Nine students out of ten, he complained, "especially in England, where so much time is given to Greek and Latin composition, never get through the philological vestibule at all, never arrive at *Alterthumswissenschaft*, which is a knowledge of the spirit and power of Greek and Roman antiquity learned from its original works."[5]

The barren routines prevailing in the elementary schools that Arnold inspected prompted him to recommend desperate remedies. The gross inadequacy of the textbooks used by the pupils aroused his earnest protests. Too often they were books compiled by charlatans, with no cultural vision and no professional skill. The pupil's reading book, he complained, "is often the only book of secular literature in his possession; it is important to do what we can to ensure its being a good one." He deplored especially the bad poetry offered in these books and quoted an example entitled "My Native Land," from a series much in vogue:

> She is a rich and rare land,
> Oh! she is a fresh and fair land,
> She is a dear and rare land,
>   This native land of mine.
> No men than hers are braver,

3 *Schools and Universities on the Continent* (Super, IV, 214).
4 *Ibid.*, p. 262.
5 *Ibid.*, p. 294.

The women's hearts ne'er waver;
I'd freely die to save her,
And think my lot divine.
[Etc.]

"When one thinks how noble and admirable a thing genuine popular poetry is," he said, "it is provoking to think that such rubbish as this should be palmed off on a poor child for it with any apparent sanction from the Education department and its grants."[6]

Arnold's concern over the absence of formative influences in the schools prompted him to recommend the inclusion of scriptural passages and the hymns of the Church. "There was no Greek school," he said, "in which Homer was not read; cannot our popular schools, with their narrow range and their jejune alimentation in secular literature, do as much for the Bible as the Greek schools did for Homer?"[7] Here again he found his most impressive examples in Germany:

The chief effect of the religious teaching, however, certainly lies in the Bible passages, and still more in the evangelical hymns, which are so abundantly learnt by heart and repeated by the children. No one could watch the faces of the children, of the girls particularly, without feeling that something in their nature responded to what they were repeating, and was moved by it. It is said that two thirds of the working classes in the best educated countries of Protestant Germany are detached from the received religion, and the inference is drawn that the religious teaching in the schools must be a vain formality. But may it not happen that chords are awakened by the Bible and hymns in German schools which remain a possession even though the course of later life may carry the German adult far away from Lutheran dogma?[8]

It was in accord with this hope for his own people that Arnold prepared and published, in 1872, *A Bible Reading for Schools*, consisting of chapters XL to LXVI of Isaiah. He had no illusions concerning the futility of expecting the Sunday schools to fulfil this important office of instruction, and he exhorted the managers of the British and Foreign schools to set a good example for other managers by providing a salutary programme

6 *Reports on Elementary Schools*, pp. 129–30.
7 *Ibid.*, pp. 151–2.
8 *Special Report on Certain Points Connected with Elementary Education in Germany, Switzerland, and France*, p. 14.

in this respect. Arnold even urged his own department to bring instruction in the literature of the Bible under the aegis of official inspection. But these efforts were futile. Arnold's own cultural aspirations ranged far beyond the feeble vision of most of the British officials to whom his reports were addressed.

Arnold's humanistic aim also inspired his editing, in 1875, of Samuel Johnson's "Six Chief *Lives*," Milton, Dryden, Swift, Addison, Pope, and Gray. In the preface of this book, he complained chiefly of the want of any significant organization in the things taught in the schools, the lack of any "well-grounded consent." He urged "a severe limitation in the number of matters taught, a severe uniformity in the line of study followed. Wide ranging, and the multiplication of matters to be investigated, belong to private study, – to the development of special aptitudes in the individual learner, and to the demands which they raise in him."[9]

Prompted by his anxiety to find better literary content for the schools, Arnold examined and reviewed Stopford Brooke's *A Primer of English Literature.*[10] Here again he urged an insistence on quality in the things to be taught – quality together with uniformity. "Once secure what is excellent to be taught, and you can hardly teach it with too much insistence, punctuality, universality. ... The Greeks used to say, ... Give us a fine thing two and three times over! And they were right."[11] It was in literature – "our own literature, English literature" – that English children were to find "the best which has been thought and said in the world."

Arnold's concern for the beneficent influence of letters should hardly surprise us, but his cultural aim was even broader in scope; it embraced the practical and the utilitarian as well as the literary studies. Human aptitudes, he said, incline men to follow one or the other of two main roads into the circle of knowledge: the study of man and his works, and the study of nature and her works.

To know himself, a man must know the capabilities and performances of the human spirit; and the value of the humanities, of *Alterthumswissenschaft*, the science of antiquity, is, that it affords for this purpose an unsurpassed source of light and stimulus ...

9 *The Six Chief Lives from Johnson's "Lives of the Poets"* (London: Macmillan & Co., 1881), p. x.
10 "Guide to English Literature," *Mixed Essays* (*Works*, Ed. de Luxe, x, 174–96).
11 *Ibid.*, pp. 174–5.

... But it is also a vital and formative knowledge to know the world, the laws which govern nature, and man as a part of nature. This the realists have perceived, and the truth of this perception, too, is inexpugnable.[12]

The precocity of these judgments is certainly remarkable. When Arnold uttered them, *The Origin of Species* had just been published. The year of its publication (1859) marked the first grant of state funds for the support of science instruction in special schools.[13] In the same year the degree in science was instituted by the University of London. These events remind us of the amazing recency of science as a recognized subject of study. In the common schools, it had heretofore been treated in a trivial and rudimentary fashion. In the popular mind it had been accorded no place in liberal education for the simple reason that it had not been recognized as liberating. With the rise of working men's "institutes" it had found a place; its inclusion there had been ignored by the opponents of lower-class education, because they regarded it as a gross, plebeian matter, quite proper for the inconsequential aims of the "institutes."[14]

But according to Arnold's theory of human aptitudes, science stood as one of the two roads to liberal knowledge. Science and letters – either branch would lead one into the same bright circle; and the seeker after culture would best succeed, he believed, by following his own peculiar bent. The circle of knowledge was too vast, and the scope of the human faculties too limited, to permit a wider preoccupation. And yet neither the humanists nor the realists were capable, from their extreme and invidious positions, of conceiving the full circle. The proof lay in the readiness of each faction to belittle that part of the field which it could not comprehend. The humanists insisted that man's access to the realm of vital knowledge was "by knowing himself, – the poetry, philosophy, his-

---

12 *Schools and Universities on the Continent* (Super, IV, 290).
13 These schools were called South Kensington Schools because the offices of the Science and Art Department, which supervised them, were located in South Kensington Street. The relegation of science and art to these special schools continued until 1899. From 1871 to 1875, The Royal Commission on Scientific Instruction, known as the Devonshire Commission, sat and eventually presented recommendations concerning the content of science instruction. In 1872, Thomas Henry Huxley was called in to reorganize the South Kensington Schools and to design the curriculum for them. The results were not successful. "Nowhere," says Archer, "was the insidious system of payment by results worked out so elaborately, and nowhere was education so completely replaced by 'cramming' " (*Secondary Education in the Nineteenth Century*, Cambridge, 1928, p. 140).
14 *Ibid.*, p. 100 ff.

tory which his spirit has created"; the realists looked rather to the facts and the laws of nature.[15]

Arnold deprecated both extreme positions. His humanism was broad and inclusive. He upheld the liberalizing power of science as well as that of letters. Only when driven to make a choice between the claims of one faction or the other would he express a preference:

But it seems to me that so long as the realists persist in cutting in two the circle of knowledge, so long do they leave for practical purposes the better portion to their rivals, and in the government of human affairs their rivals will beat them. And for this reason. The study of letters is the study of the operation of human force, of human freedom and activity; the study of nature is the study of the operation of non-human forces, of human limitation and passivity. The contemplation of human force and activity tends naturally to heighten our own force and activity; the contemplation of human limits and passivity tends rather to check it.[16]

From the perspective of a scientific era which Arnold never lived to enter, the argument may appear to be somewhat naïve. It reveals a polemic, a rationalistic, habitude of mind, one that settles issues dialectically.[17] And yet it is clear that Arnold, standing on the very threshold of the scientific age, understood its experimental temper, and shared its aspirations and ideals. His friendship for Huxley was touching in its deference and genuine solicitude. The two were fellow members of the Athenaeum Club, and they conversed with genuine camaraderie and affection. Writing to his sister "K" in 1884, Arnold said of the great lecturer: "He is very ill, and looks like a man quite spent. I have a real affection for him though we seldom meet; it brought tears into my eyes to see him. But I should think he would have great rallying power, when he gets real rest."[18]

Even Huxley's agnosticism did not repel Arnold. A charming passage from the Preface to *St. Paul and Protestantism* shows Arnold's willingness to intercede for him: "Give the churches of Nonconformity free scope, cries an ardent Congregationalist, and we will renew the wonders of the first times; we will confront this modern bugbear of physical science,

---

15 *Schools and Universities on the Continent* (Super, IV, 290–3). Cf. Connell, chap. VIII.

16 *Schools and Universities on the Continent* (Super, IV, 292).

17 Cf. Walter J. Hipple, Jr., "Matthew Arnold, Dialectician," *University of Toronto Quarterly*, XXXII (October 1962), 5–6.

18 *Unpublished Letters*, p. 54.

show how hollow she is, and how she contradicts herself! In his mind's eye, this Nonconforming enthusiast already sees Professor Huxley in a white sheet, brought up at the Surrey Tabernacle between two deacons ... and penitently confessing that *Science contradicts herself*."[19] The often-mentioned controversy between Arnold and Huxley was nothing more than an amicable clarification, the shoring up of a basic agreement. Each defended his own discipline, to be sure, but each also made a substantial high-minded apologia for the other's cultural importance. Arnold's defence of science has been quoted above (pp. 103–4). Huxley's statement on behalf of classical studies was made before the South London Working Men's College in 1868:

Now, do not expect me to depreciate the earnest and enlightened pursuit of classical learning. I have not the least desire to speak ill of such occupations, nor any sympathy with those who run them down. On the contrary, if my opportunities had lain in that direction, there is no investigation into which I could have thrown myself with greater delight than that of antiquity.

What science can present greater attractions than philology? How can a lover of literary excellence fail to rejoice in the ancient masterpieces? ... Classical history is a great section of the palaeontology of man; and I have the same double respect for it as for other kinds of palaeontology – that is to say, a respect for the facts which it establishes as for all facts, and a still greater respect for it as a preparation for the discovery of a law of progress.[20]

Huxley deplored, just as Arnold did,[21] the dull, uninspired teaching of the classics which he witnessed in the schools. He well knew the meaning of the stultifying rigours of "the philological vestibule."

It means getting up endless forms and rules by heart. It means turning Latin and Greek into English, for the mere sake of being able to do it, and without the smallest regard to the worth, or worthlessness, of the author read. It means the learning of innumerable, not always decent, fables in such a shape that the meaning they once had is dried up into utter trash; and the only impression left upon the boy's mind is, that the

19 *St. Paul and Protestantism* (Super, VI, 127). A similar intervention occurs in *Culture and Anarchy* (Super, V, 103).
20 "A Liberal Education and Where to Find It," *Collected Essays* (New York, 1897), III, 97–8.
21 See pp. 101–2, *supra*.

people who believed such things must have been the greatest idiots the world ever saw.[22]

Between the respective cultural ideals of the two men there was general agreement. They observed the self-same educational problems – from different sides, it is true, but each with the same genuine solicitude for all liberal studies. Both were exponents of the same true culture; both yearned steadily toward the same bright cynosure. An interesting correspondence between the two had been revealed by Professor W. H. G. Armytage. One detail of it is most significant here; in the letter of 17 October 1880, Arnold made this comment:

What you say of me is abundantly kind, and God forbid that I should make such a bad return as to enter into controversy with you: but I will remark that the dictum about knowing "the best that has been known and said in the world" was meant to include knowing what has been said in science and art as well as letters. I remember changing the word *said* to the word *uttered*, because I was dissatisfied with the formula for seeming not to include art, and a picture or a statue may be called an *utterance* though it cannot be called a *saying*: however I went back to *said* for the base reason that the formula runs so much easier off the tongue with the shorter word. But I never doubted that the formula included science.[23]

The depth and persistence of Arnold's commitment to the study of science emerges clearly from a reading of his letters and education reports. He looked upon science especially as the paramount need of the rising middle class, a class now brought up on the second plane, insufferably and arrogantly proud of its own inanities. "If only, in compensation, it had science, systematic knowledge! The stronghold of science should naturally be in a nation's middle class, who have neither luxury nor bodily toil to bar them from it. But here comes in the intellectual inconvenience of the bad condition of the mass of our secondary schools. ... Short as the offspring of our public schools and universities come of the idea of science and systematic knowledge, the offspring of our middle class academies probably come, if that be possible, even shorter."[24]

Arnold's devotion to science as a humanizing study places him among

22 Huxley, pp. 100–1.
23 W. H. G. Armytage, "Matthew Arnold and T. H. Huxley: Some New Letters, 1870–80," *Review of English Studies*, IV, N.S. (1953), 346–53.
24 *Schools and Universities on the Continent* (Super, IV, 309).

the frontier educators of his time. Many have spoken of his conservatism, of the conflicts that encumbered his moral judgment, of his tendency to uphold old forms and customs against the onslaught of the liberal powers of reform.[25] Such judgments overlook one of his most impressive traits. Begin where one may in the study of his work, there is immediately evident the habit of the investigative mind. As early as his inaugural lecture from the Chair of poetry at Oxford (1857), he upheld the importance of the inductive approach to understanding. In this lecture he spoke of a "second deliverance" – "an intellectual deliverance." The demand for it arises, he said, "because the present age exhibits to the individual man who contemplates it the spectacle of a vast multitude of facts awaiting and inviting his comprehension. The deliverance consists in man's comprehension of this present and past. It begins when our mind begins to enter into possession of the general ideas which are the law of this vast multitude of facts."[26] A gathering of the facts, and a disinterested reflection thereon – these give us the measure of his intellect. In his essay on Sainte-Beuve, he recognized this scientific habit of thought and proclaimed it as his great exemplar's literary ideal: "His curiosity was unbounded, and he was a born *naturalist*, carrying into letters, so often the mere domain of rhetoric and futile amusement, the ideas and methods of scientific natural inquiry. ... he strove to find the real data with which, in dealing with man and his affairs, we have to do. Beyond this study he did not go, – to find the real data."[27]

Though Arnold's formal education had been, of course, in the classical tradition, he had absorbed from somewhere the spirit of the new science as well – a spirit which had invaded the intellectual life of Oxford as a kind of second movement. Louis Bonnerot has stated well its all-pervading genius:

Ce second mouvement diffère du premier en ceci qu'il se détache de l'orthodoxie, se laisse pénétrer par l'exégèse et la métaphysique allemandes et reflète ainsi l'esprit nouveau, c'est-à-dire l'idée d'évolution. Cette idée est l'idée maîtresse du siècle; elle triomphe grâce à Spencer

25 See, for example, Patrick J. McCarthy, *Matthew Arnold and the Three Classes* (New York, 1964), chap. III; Edward Clarence Mack, *Public Schools and British Opinion since 1860* (New York, 1941), pp. 68–9; Lionel Trilling, *Matthew Arnold* (New York, 1939), pp. 278 ff.; Alexander Meiklejohn, *Education between Two Worlds* (New York, 1942), p. 47 ff.
26 "On the Modern Element in Literature" (Super, I, 20).
27 Super, v, 306.

et à Darwin, dont *The Origin of Species* paraît en 1859, mais elle existait déjà en germe chez Tennyson, Newman, et, avant eux, chez Goethe. C'est, je l'ai déjà dit, à ce dernier, qu'Arnold l'emprunta et c'est du Zeit-Geist, du Time-Spirit, c'est-à-dire de la loi du développement et du changement, qu'Arnold fit le principe central de sa philosophie religieuse, parce qu'il la trouva en conformité avec sa notion intuitive du mouvant.[28]

Because of his faith in the civilizing power of science, Arnold also sought to broaden the scope of its inclusion within the studies of the elementary school. In his report to the Committee of Council for the year 1878, he re-emphasized especially the importance of this branch of study:

> In my last report [1876] I proposed that what the Germans call *Naturkunde* [Huxley's common term was *Erdkunde*] – some knowledge of the facts and laws of nature – should be taught as a class-subject[29] in addition to grammar, geography, and English history. ... The excuse for putting most of these matters into our programme is that we are all coming to be agreed that an entire ignorance of the system of nature is as gross a defect in our children's education as not to know that there ever was such a person as Charles the First. Now our ordinary class-programme provides, or at any rate suggests, some remedy against the second kind of ignorance, for history is one of our class-subjects;[30] it provides none against the first. This is a blot; we ought surely to provide that some knowledge of the system of nature should form part of the regular course.[31]

Readers of the *Letters* may recall that in his correspondence with his youngest sister "Fan," he seldom failed to mention some plant he had

28 Bonnerot, p. 248.
29 By 1867, the dessicating effects of the Revised Code – in drawing all instructional attention to the grant-earning subjects of reading, writing, and arithmetic – had become so critical that the Committee of Council issued a Minute instituting an additional grant dependent, among other conditions, upon the inclusion of "one or more specific subjects of secular instruction." In his report for 1867, Arnold mentioned language, geography, and history, and said that "the Minute of last February, which makes them subjects of a grant-bringing examination has, by recalling attention to them, made manifest into what decay they had sunk" (*Reports on Elementary Schools*, p. 123).
30 The Minute of 1867 required the offering of only one or more of these subjects in the schools and did not specify which should be favoured.
31 *Reports on Elementary Schools*, pp. 204–6.

seen in his customary walks, usually giving the scientific name. "Tell Fan," he wrote to his mother, "the slopes of the clay cliff were covered with the wild parsnip, its broad hats of yellow honey-coloured flowers very rich and tempting. Tell her I have also found out that the Essex plant I thought was hemlock is the sheep's parsley; and the true hemlock I have discovered near Harrow, such a handsome plant, and quite unmistakable when you have once seen it. I will take her straight to it when she comes to us next spring. Mr. Gibson has sent me another copy of his *Essex Flora*. I had given away the first, so I am getting quite a botanical library."[32] One of his chief interests on his visits abroad, especially in America, was the character of the native flora, particularly its likenesses with, and differences from, the species he had studied as an amateur botanist on his own English countryside.

Arnold's concern for science as a part of the programme for schools certainly arose from a genuine faith in its cultural power. His solicitude for natural knowledge differed not at all in kind, but only in degree, from his devotion for literature itself. The trait he had early recognized and admired in Sainte-Beuve was indeed an aspect of his own self-image which he found reflected in another mind. He called this trait "curiosity, – a desire after the things of the mind simply for their own sakes and for the pleasure of seeing them as they are, – which is, in an intelligent being, natural and laudable."[33] Such curiosity is, in fact, indispensable to the poet – the maker of literature – and Arnold, possessing it himself, understood its importance for others. He distinguished this trait also as constituting the excellent gift of Maurice de Guérin. In his comment on Guérin, indeed, one may discern Arnold's notion of the superiority of the poetic, over the utilitarian depiction of nature – both of them depending, however, upon the acute observation of things as they are:

The interpretations of science do not give us this intimate sense of objects as the interpretations of poetry give it; they appeal to a limited faculty, and not to the whole man. It is not Linnaeus or Cavendish or Cuvier who gives us the sense of animals, or water, or plants, who seizes their secret for us, who makes us participate in their life; it is Shakespeare, with his   *daffodils*
> *That come before the swallow dares, and take*
> *The winds of March with beauty;*

32 *Letters*, II, 33–4 (June 16, 1870).
33 *Culture and Anarchy* (Super, v, 91).

it is Wordsworth, with his   *voice ... heard*
     In spring-time from the cuckoo-bird,
     Breaking the silence of the seas
     Among the farthest Hebrides;

it is Keats, with his   *moving waters at their priest-like task*
     Of cold ablution round Earth's human shores;

it is Chateaubriand, with his *"cîme indéterminée des forêts"*; it is Senan-
cour, with his mountain birch-tree: *"Cette écorce blanche, lisse et cre-
vassée; cette tige agreste; ces branches qui s'inclinent vers la terre; la
mobilité des feuilles, et tout cet abandon, simplicité de la nature, attitude
des déserts."*[34]

It is, in short, the power of the imagination superadded to all that the
exacting descriptive naturalist is able to depict.

The importance of the realistic side of education is never denied by
Arnold. An illuminating example of his inner unfettered judgment
occurs in a letter of January 1866, written to his sister "K":

If it is *perception* you want to cultivate in Florence[35] you had much
better take some science (botany is perhaps the best for a girl, and I
know Tyndall thinks it the best of all for educational purposes), and
choosing a good handbook, go regularly through it with her. ... I cannot
see that there is much got out of learning the Latin Grammar except the
mainly normal discipline of learning something much more exactly than
one is made to learn anything else; and the verification of the laws of
grammar, in the examples furnished by one's reading, is certainly a far
less fruitful stimulus of one's powers of observation and comparison than
the verification of the laws of a science like botany in the examples furnished by the world of nature before one's eyes. The sciences have been
abominably taught, and by untrained people, but the moment properly
trained people begin to teach them properly they fill such a want in

34 "Maurice de Guérin" (Super, III, 13).
35 One of the four children of William Delafield Arnold, a brother of Matthew
   and Mrs. Forster. William died at Gibraltar on 9 April 1859 while on his way
   home from India (see *Letters*, I, 79–80, April 14, 1859). His wife having
   died in India a year earlier, the Forsters adopted the four orphans after
   William's death (Reid, I, 316–7).

education as that which you feel in Florence's better than either grammar or mathematics, which have been forced into the service because they have been hitherto so far better studied and known.[36]

Here, as he ministers unto his own with a judgment unencumbered by the conditions that perplex the friends of popular education, we may apprehend his true opinions. At the apex of his dream stood the two great humanizing studies, fostering severally the two main aptitudes by means of which man gains access to his vital and formative knowledge; the one leading him to study man and his works, the other to study nature and her works. Within this fascinating circle, he comprehended all that could be implied by the word "liberal," all that could illumine and ennoble man in society. There is a kind of largess, an expansive benignity in his affection for these things, an idealistic fervour that would exclude from his garden of the mind all mean and pedantic things.

In 1879 Arnold collected into a new volume a number of his earlier essays, including one, his "Democracy," which he had written to preface his first foreign report. Seeking to explain the unifying tendency of these *Mixed Essays*, he presented in his preface a theory of literature as a civilizing power – literature being of itself only a part of civilization, not the whole. "What then," asked Arnold, "is civilisation, which some people seem to conceive of as if it meant railroads and the penny post, and little more ... ? Civilisation is the humanisation of man in society. Man is civilised when the whole body of society comes to live with a life worthy to be called *human*, and corresponding to man's true aspirations and powers." And among the means by which this happy state was to be attained, the familiar power of *expansion* stood at the pinnacle of importance. That basic principle being given, he proceeded to enumerate the other powers by which man's humanization was to be achieved: "They are the power of conduct, the power of intellect and knowledge, the power of beauty, the power of social life and manners. Expansion, conduct, science, beauty, manners, – here are the conditions of civilisation, the claimants which man must satisfy before he can be humanised."[37] If one were to seek a single unifying principle encompassing all that Arnold ever said about schools and the curriculum, one could do no better than to seize upon this.

All the efforts of his lifetime centre about one master motive: "a con-

36 *Letters*, I, 313–14 (Sunday, January 1866). See also *Letters*, II, 83–4 (May 8, 1872), for another comment on the relative value of grammar.
37 Preface to *Mixed Essays* (*Works*, Ed. de Luxe, x, vi–ix.).

cern for civilization, for the 'humanisation of man in society,' for the building of a culture in which 'the whole body of society comes to live with a life worthy to be called *human,* and corresponding to man's true aspirations and powers.' "[38] In its essence this unifying theme was democratic, for it envisioned the ultimate self-realization of all men through the power of human expansion within a milieu made favourable to human growth. The reforms that he proposed were offered in the spirit of this master aim. They were visionary but not nebulous. The chaos of educational mismanagement that he beheld was truly maddening. It was a product of planlessness – the confused flux of many independent efforts, worthy and laudable in themselves, but maintained and fostered by jealous competing agencies, each with a vested interest to protect. The institution of state grants in 1833 had not allayed, but only intensified the inherent conflicts; it had subsidized – under proper safeguards, it is true – the enterprises of jealous factions. Within the general destitution, moreover, private venture schools of questionable character were bound to flourish. Arnold had seen them and had deplored their deceptive, mercenary enticements. Ambitious parents of the middle class, now coming into possession of the means of supplying education for their children, were especially susceptible to educational frauds and blackguardism. Dickens' descriptions of contemporary private schools are not malicious caricatures. Arnold himself testified to the accuracy of their depiction. Writing to his friend and fellow inspector, Sir Joshua Fitch, in 1880, he said, "I have this year been reading *David Copperfield* for the first time. Mr. Creakle's school at Blackheath is the type of our ordinary middle class schools, and our middle class is satisfied that so it should be."[39]

The correction of such abuses depended, as Arnold clearly saw, upon the determined intervention of the state. His plan for their correction was an adaptation to English conditions, with concessions to the distinctive English temperament, of what he had seen working successfully in Germany, Switzerland, Holland, and Italy. In his report to the Schools Inquiry Commission, not only did he re-enjoin his countrymen, but he outlined the very form and structure that he thought the organization of national education should take. First of all, there must be an Education Minister, not only as an administrative convenience, but as *"a centre in which to fix responsibility."* Second, in order to assist and advise the

38 Hipple, p. 4.

39 *Letters,* ii, 184 (October 14, 1880). See also Dickens' description of the Yorkshire schools in the Preface to *Nicholas Nickleby.* Cp. p. 52, *supra,* note 44.

Education Minister, Arnold would create a High Council of Education such as existed in France and Italy – a consultative body consisting, not of political personages, but of professional leaders chosen for their known expertness in special branches of educational affairs. The third feature of the administrative hierarchy would be provincial school boards, such as he had seen in Germany. Eight or ten such boards, each consisting of not more than five or six members, one being paid, should administer the educational enterprise for the whole country. Each board would represent the state in the country, keeping the Education Minister informed of the conditions prevailing within the districts and serving as a direct liaison between the Minister and local school officials. The boards would see to the execution of all public regulations which applied to the schools, visiting the schools as often as necessary and representing the state at the main annual examinations. The provincial boards, should, in fact, obviate the need for an elaborate system of inspection, a function that Arnold considered "neither requisite nor desirable" on the secondary level.[40]

This simple tripartite administrative organization would constitute the entire regulative machinery of the state. Beginning at once to exercise its control within the clearly designated spheres of governmental responsibility, it would draw the whole body of British secondary schools within its ambit. "Where," asked Arnold, "are the English higher schools ... with which this Minister, this Council, and these School Boards are to deal? All of his experience gleaned in observing the schools of foreign countries pointed to one clear answer: "Wherever there is a school-endowment, there is a right of public supervision, and, if necessary, of a resettlement of the endowment by public authority. Wherever, again, there is a school endowment from the Crown or the State, there is a right, to the State, of participation in the management of the endowment, and of representation on the body which manages it."[41] Even the public schools might

40 *Schools and Universities on the Continent* (Super, IV, 314–16).
41 *Ibid.*, p. 316. The problem of obsolete, malfunctioning endowments had haunted English educational leaders ever since Henry Brougham (Baron Brougham and Vaux), on 20 June 1816, had proposed before the House of Commons the appointment of a commission to investigate the shocking abuses that had come to the attention of his Select Committee to Inquire into the State of the Education of the Lower Orders of the People in London, Westminster, and Southwark. Among many other instances, Brougham had cited "one flagrant case where 1,500 *l.* which was left for the endowment of a school, was managed by the lord of the manor, who appointed his own brother schoolmaster with a large salary, while he again shifted the duties to a deputy

be absorbed within the state system. Some of them, like Eton, Westminster, and Christ's Hospital, were originally royal foundations. The right of the state to share in the administration of these schools could easily be defended. Others of them, schools like Winchester, Rugby, and Harrow, while not royal foundations, were nevertheless foundation schools, to which the right of public supervision would apply.

The form of control which the state would exercise over these institutions would simply be a supervision of the main examinations through the provincial boards or through members of the High Council of Education. Upon the results of these examinations would depend the right of matriculation at the universities and access to the higher positions in the public service. The pupils of all private schools would be allowed to undergo the same examinations; and thus, directly or indirectly, every secondary school in the land would be brought within the governance of the High Council of Education.[42]

Certainly these are not the judgments of a traditionalist, a defender of things as they are; they are the studied, constructive counsels of the seasoned liberal, speaking from a broadening experience within his own country, as well as from his extensive observations abroad. Neither may they be dissevered from the milieu of current political and social affairs. To suggest so, as some critics have done, is to overlook entirely Arnold's habitual preoccupations with temporal matters – as when, at the age of thirty-seven, he stood on the soil of France, an English official on an educational mission. On that occasion Arnold clearly demonstrated his inability to dissociate the educational from the political problem. Indeed, he turned his attention first of all to the latter – then the all-absorbing interest – and laid the political groundwork upon which he thought the educational structure must rest.

The truth is that Arnold stood in the full current of the democratic movements of the century, not as a reluctant or obstructive agent, but as a prime mover for popular reform. Tested by this constant, pervasive principle, there is no conflict in his political motives as distinguished from his educational vision. In his characteristic zeal for democratic

----

schoolmaster, in the person of a joiner, with the small income of 40 *l.* a year, and left this ignorant person to educate the children" (Hansard, *The Parliamentary Debates from the Year 1803 to the Present Time*, xxxiv, 1233). Arnold's recommendations of 1866 substantiate remarkably the principles for which Brougham had fought fifty years earlier, and suffered ignominious defeat.

42 *Schools and Universities on the Continent*, pp. 317–18.

reform, he looked to the perfection of a state system of public education as the indispensable means. Herein lies the strong thread of his unwavering consistency. The just gratification of the universal instincts of humanity – the instinct for *expansion* and the instinct for *equality* – was to be had in no other way.

What, then, was the motive, so deeply implanted in Arnold's nature, that held him to this constant conviction? It was a steadfast clinging to that which is good. With Burke he shared a horror of the chaotic destruction of the cultural heritage at the hands of the mob. He would not condone the rioting in Hyde Park, but neither would he oust the Philistine from participation in political affairs. *"Force till right is ready,"* he had said earlier, quoting Joubert: " 'C'est la force et le droit qui règlent toutes choses dans le monde: la force en attendant le droit.' (Force and right are the governors of this world; force till right is ready.) ... and till right is ready, force, the existing order of things, is justified, is the legitimate ruler."[43] Arnold held the rule of the people devoutly to be wished, but such a rule must await and accompany the universal diffusion of culture. This latter office the state must undertake as its own special obligation, and in the meantime the Philistine must be judiciously restrained.

The desire to preserve and to strengthen that which is good is the generic concept of the term *conservatism*. It is also the motive, often, of the world's great liberals; and Arnold, who invariably called himself a liberal, stood steadfastly on that platform. There was, it is true, much in Arnold's nature that made Establishment attractive. Speaking in the preface to *Culture and Anarchy* of the narrowness, the one-sidedness,, the incompleteness, the *provinciality* of the Nonconformists, he enunciated clearly his faith in the unifying, long-abiding institutions of mankind's hereditary culture:

The great works by which, not only in literature, art, and science generally, but in religion itself, the human spirit has manifested its approaches to totality and to full, harmonious perfection, and by which it stimulates and helps forward the world's general perfection, come, not from Nonconformists, but from men who either belong to Establishments or have been trained in them. ... The believer in machinery may think that to get a Government to abolish Church-rates or to legalise marriage with a deceased wife's sister is to exert a moral and ennobling influence upon Government. But a lover of perfection, who looks to inward ripeness for the true springs of conduct, will surely think that as Shakespeare

43 "The Function of Criticism at the Present Time" (Super, III, 265–6).

has done more for the inward ripeness of our statesmen than Dr. Watts, and has, therefore, done more to moralise and ennoble them, so an Establishment which has produced Hooker, Barrow, Butler, has done more to moralise and ennoble English statesmen and their conduct than communities which have produced the Nonconformist divines. The fruitful men of English Puritanism and Nonconformity are men who were trained within the pale of the Establishment, – Milton, Baxter, Wesley. A generation or two outside the Establishment, and Puritanism produces men of national mark no more.[44]

Now here are dicta which press close upon the passions and prejudices of men; surely they strike squarely athwart the sentiments of radical men and invite upon their author the censure of *conservatism*. But the fact is that Arnold, calling himself a liberal, prophesied and welcomed the rise of the common man. At a time when his countrymen were terrified by the apparition of a revolutionary France, Arnold expressed a congenial admiration for the spirit of that nation's "idea-moved masses," and for the democratic essence that pervaded the land. When, in *England and the Italian Question,* he said of Louis Napoleon that *"he possesses, largely and deeply interwoven in his constitution, the popular fibre,"* he was expressing what his own spiritual antennae had enabled him sympathetically to determine. In his own nature there was the same quick perception, the same animistic chord vibrating with the popular *pneuma*.

And finally, late in life, at a time when the spirit of caution settles comfortably upon the minds of many men, Arnold could still utter this reflection for the solace of his younger colleagues who had gathered to do him honour:

My reflection is one to comfort and cheer myself, and I hope others, at this our parting. We are entering upon new times, where many influences, once potent to guide and restrain, are failing. Some people think the prospect of the reign of democracy, as they call it, very gloomy. This is unwise, but no one can regard it quite without anxiety. It is nearly 150 years since the wisest of English clergymen told the Lord Mayor and Sheriffs of London in a hospital sermon that the poor are very much what the rich make them. (Hear, hear.) That is profoundly true, though perhaps it rather startles us to hear it.[45]

44 *Culture and Anarchy* (Super, v, 237–8).
45 From a farewell speech at a dinner given by the teachers of Westminster upon the occasion of Arnold's resignation as inspector of schools, recorded in the (London) *Times*, 13 November 1886, and never republished until 1960, in Neiman's *Essays, Letters, and Reviews,* pp. 306–11.

Surely, with these words of the aging Arnold, the persistent spirit of progress is again vindicated.

It was at violence, at wanton destruction, at blind precipitate action that Arnold rebelled; thence emanated his antipathy to Philistine claptrap, to arrogant self-assertion, to the obstinate insistence upon the unbounded right to do exactly as one pleased. In the experience of the race, there lay, he believed, a fountain of empirical wisdom, an "establishment" of practical polity, ready for the sustenance and guidance of man in all of his social undertakings. This, he thought, it would be folly to ignore. Let the common man drink deeply from this spring, and then let him govern.

This was Arnold's message to his people; and in urging this platform, together with the clear outline of an enabling plan, he was steadfast and persistent. When weighing this fact, one finds that a special attention to the single decade of the 1860s is wonderfully impressive when considered as a period of trial. Witness the crushing triumph of "The Revised Code" – its desolating reversal of an imminent renaissance within the schools, its adamantine finality. This catastrophe occurred in the very midst of Arnold's fresh awakening – just after he had published his *Popular Education of France* and its prefatory essay, "Democracy." His writing of *A French Eton* was delayed by his response to the new emergency. And yet the tenor of his constructive thought throughout the period remained clear and steady. It suffered no discouragement and brooked no overthrow. It rose, rather, in a strong vigorous crescendo throughout the decade, reaching its grand climax in 1869.

The cardinal tenets of his thought have been already delineated: (1) the brooding influence of the popular will; (2) the waning genteel governance of the old aristocracy; (3) the pressing national need to enlighten the new holders of the franchise; (4) the necessity to rely more and more upon the benevolent action of the state; and (5) the imminent and wished-for fusion of the old social classes through the dissemination of culture.[46]

Of these five concepts, it was the third and fourth that were salient; for they represented the practical, the instrumental aspects of reform. They were, besides, the concepts most often in Arnold's mind; for they would encompass the reduction of the current emergency, and together they constituted the key to his consistent speculation on social and educational affairs. They pointed also to a problem that Arnold understood as peculiarly British in character, one that originated in a purely British

46 See p. 58, *supra*.

foible and one that afflicted the British people as a distinctly national disease. It was these concepts, in fact, that Arnold selected from his official report to the Newcastle Commission and chose to expand and illuminate in his separate report to the nation;[47] they became, in fact, the central theme of the introductory essay, "Democracy," which Arnold wrote to prepare the general reader to receive his personal message: "On what action may we rely, to replace, for some time at any rate, that action of the aristocracy upon the people of this country, which we have seen exercise an influence in many respects elevating and beneficial, but which is rapidly, and from inevitable causes, ceasing? ... I confess I am disposed to answer: On the action of the State."[48]

Arnold knew of course that in such an advocacy he would be touching a point of extreme British sensitivity, and that he must hasten to draw a distinction and to allay the expected misapprehension:

If I were a Frenchman I should never be weary of admiring the independent, individual, local habits and action in England, of directing attention to the evils occasioned in France by the excessive action of the State; for I should be very sure that, say what I might, the part of the State would never be too small in France, nor that of the individual too large. Being an Englishman, I see nothing but good in freely recognising the coherence, rationality, and efficaciousness which characterise the strong State-action of France, of acknowledging the want of method, reason, and result which attend the feeble State-action of England; because I am very sure that, strengthen in England the action of the State as one may, it will always find itself sufficiently controlled.[49]

Nor, he continued, have the English people, with their boasted freedom to do exactly as they please, any resultant achievements to which they may look with pride. Their cultural aspirations have remained quiescent and undeveloped; England stands before the world as a cultural failure. Her condition is distinctly a middle-class, a Philistine failure, directly

---

47 After the publication of the official report of the Newcastle Commission, containing Arnold's *Popular Education of France with Notices of That of Holland and Switzerland* (in vol. IV), he received permission to republish his own report as a personal venture (see *Letters*, I, 127, December 17, 1860). According to Super, the only other assistant commissioner to issue a separate report was Patrick Cumin, on educational charities (vol. II, "Critical and Explanatory Notes," p. 330).

48 Super, II, 15–16.

49 *Ibid.*, pp. 16–17.

traceable to her much-vaunted prerogative, to the national propensity for doing exactly as one pleases, to an intolerance of authority.

English democracy runs no risk of being overmastered by the State; it is almost certain that it will throw off the tutelage of aristocracy. Its real danger is, that it will have far too much its own way, and be left far too much to itself. "What harm will there be in that?" say some; "are we not a self-governing people?" I answer: "We have never yet been a *self-governing democracy*, or anything like it." The difficulty for democracy is, how to find and keep high ideals. The individuals who compose it are, the bulk of them, persons who need to follow an ideal, not to set one; and one ideal of greatness, high feeling, and fine culture, which an aristocracy once supplied to them, they lose by the very fact of ceasing to be a lower order and becoming a democracy. Nations are not truly great solely because the individuals composing them are numerous, free, and active; but they are great when these numbers, this freedom, and this activity are employed in the service of an ideal higher than that of an ordinary man, taken by himself. Our society is probably destined to become much more democratic; who or what will give a high tone to the nation then? That is the grave question.[50]

The corrective that Arnold proposed was to be the prime concern, the dedicated aim of all national effort, namely, the fostering of a broad and generous culture, "an endeavour to come at right reason and the will of God by means of reading, observing, thinking," "culture being a pursuit of our total perfection by means of getting to know on all matters which most concern us, the best which has been thought and said in the world." In proposing this one expedient, Arnold was labouring under no illusions as to the difficulty of the method – the long, patient cultivation required, the necessity of lifting the whole mass of society together rather than any favoured segment. There is at the close of his report on the educational system of France a passage which seems at first to repudiate the very principle of national education, which seems to reverse what Arnold elsewhere always maintained as a fundamental requisite for the regeneration of the English people. The passage puzzles the reader until he seizes its almost cryptic import. Arnold had seen in France a system that was inadequate but unpretentious, one that fixed a low level of popular instruction certainly, but one that was indigenous and responsive to the genius of the people. In England, on the other hand, he saw a system not national, one that had done much for superior primary instruction, but

50 *Ibid.*, pp. 17–18.

for elementary primary instruction very little indeed. Of this system he said:

That it may accomplish something important for the latter [elementary primary instruction], some have conceived the project of making it national. Against this project there are, it seems to me, grave objections. It is a grave objection, that the system is over-centralised – that it is too negligent of local machinery – that it is inordinately expensive. It is a graver, that to make it national would be to make national a system not salutary to the national character in the very points where that character most needs a salutary corrective; a system which, to the loud blasts of unreason and intolerance, sends forth no certain counterblast; which submissively accompanies the hatefulest and most barren of all kinds of dispute, religious dispute, into its smallest channels; – stereotypes every crotchet, every prejudice, every division, by recognising it; and suggests to its recipients no higher rationality than it finds in them.[51]

In all the countries which Arnold had visited for the Newcastle Commission – France, Holland, Switzerland – he had found national education established upon sound cultural principles; it might have been inadequate, but never degenerate. Each government had made an effectual rapprochement with its considerable religious factions by establishing a co-operative plan of religious instruction.[52] Each restricted the teaching of religion in its lay schools to the priests and ministers of its various communions, inviting them into the schools at definitely stated intervals for that purpose. The guarantees of religious accommodation were secured by statute. In England, on the other hand, all but the British and Foreign schools were rigidly denominational, either avowedly exclusive, or bent upon proselytizing the children who were of other persuasions. Besides these denominational schools, wrapped up in their petty prejudices, there were the schools of the Philistine commercial groups – particularly offensive to Arnold – schools of the Licensed Victuallers or the Commercial Travellers, "ordinary men, with their natural taste for the bathos still strong," determined to bring up their children, "not only at home but at school too, in a kind of odour of licensed victualism or of bagmanism."[53] Then there were the schools and institutes for working men, like the newly founded American university of Mr. Ezra Cornell,

51 *Ibid.*, pp. 164–5.
52 Brief explanations of these arrangements may be found in Super, II, as follows: for France, pp. 83–5; for Switzerland, p. 168; and for Holland, pp. 202–3.
53 *Culture and Anarchy* (Super, v, 154).

"a really noble monument of his munificence," yet resting, seemingly, "on a misconception of what culture truly is, and to be calculated to produce miners, or engineers, or architects, not sweetness and light."[54]

Arnold did not propose to nationalize the narrowness, the one-sidedness, the incompleteness of these Philistine patterns, but rather to perfect them and refine them by means of a superior cultural control. Then – after the renovation, but not before – with the ideal state established in authority, might come the nationalization of the schools. His solution was offered in his report of 1861, but it is also stated, and better phrased, in *Culture and Anarchy*:

Well, then, what if we tried to rise above the idea of class to the idea of the whole community, *the State*, and to find our centre of light and authority there? Every one of us has the idea of country, as a sentiment; hardly any one of us has the idea of *the State*, as a working power. And why? Because we habitually live in our ordinary selves, which do not carry us beyond the ideas and wishes of the class to which we happen to belong. And we are all afraid of giving to the State too much power, because we only conceive of the State as something equivalent to the class in occupation of the executive government, and are afraid of that class abusing power to its own purposes. ... By our everyday selves, however, we are separate, personal, at war; we are only safe from one another's tyranny when no one has any power; and this safety, in its turn, cannot save us from anarchy. And when, therefore, anarchy presents itself as a danger to us, we know not where to turn.

But by our *best self* we are united, impersonal, at harmony. We are in no peril from giving authority to this, because it is the truest friend we all of us can have; and when anarchy is a danger to us, to this authority we may turn with sure trust. Well, and this is the very self which culture, or the study of perfection, seeks to develop in us; at the expense of our old untransformed self, taking pleasure only in doing what it likes or is used to do, and exposing us to the risk of clashing with every one else who is doing the same! So that our poor culture, which is flouted as so unpractical, leads us to the very ideas capable of meeting the great want of our present embarrassed times! We want an authority, and we find nothing but jealous classes, checks, and a dead-lock; culture suggests the idea of *the State*. We find no basis for a firm State-power in our ordinary selves; culture suggests one to us in our *best self*.[55]

54 *Ibid.*, pp. 244–5.
55 *Ibid.*, pp. 134–5.

THE CHARACTER OF ARNOLD'S INTELLECTUAL LIBERALISM

It is clear, now, that Arnold's concept of the state is somewhat mystic; it was based not on actuality but on the substance of things hoped for.[56] Instead of "jealous classes, checks, and a dead-lock," he would impose the benevolent action of the state; though its animus would arise out of the will of the *demos*, it would be the embodiment of "our best self," as contradistinguished from our prejudiced, blundering, ordinary self. Such a benevolent authority would usher in the establishment of man's accumulated culture, his inherited social wisdom, "right reason and the will of God." To such an apotheosis Arnold would entrust the control of human institutions – the Church, the school, the political power.

Arnold believed that he had seen a practical working example of such a benevolent power. On his second mission to the Continent, in Prussia, under the most autocratic of governments, he had found a most effectual educational structure, a system adapted to the needs of the middle class. Many of the Prussian schools had been instituted by the Crown and were maintained in large part by Crown patronage. All were under the control of a central authority, the Minister of Education, and all were integrated with the national universities through the powers of inspection and the training and licensing of teachers. Looking sadly toward home, Arnold observed that "on the Continent the middle class in general may be said to be brought up *on the first plane*, while in England it is brought up *on the second plane*. In the public higher schools of Prussia or France 65,000 of the youth of the middle and upper classes are brought up; in the public higher schools of England, – even when we reckon as such many institutions which would not be entitled to such rank on the Continent, – only some 15,000. Has this state of things no bad effect upon us?"[57]

Accordingly, in *Culture and Anarchy*, Arnold recalls the Crown schools of Prussia in support of his major premise:

In Prussia, the best schools are Crown patronage schools, as they are called: schools which have been established and endowed (and new ones are to this day being established and endowed) by the Sovereign himself

56 Lionel Trilling traces this Platonic theory of the ideal state to Arnold's father, Dr. Thomas Arnold (*Matthew Arnold*, pp. 51–6). See also Frank J. W. Harding's comment in note 51, p. 55, *supra*.

57 *Schools and Universities on the Continent* (Super, IV, 28).

out of his own revenues, to be under the direct control and management of him or of those representing him, and to serve as types of what schools should be. The Sovereign, as his position raises him above many prejudices and littlenesses, and as he can always have at his disposal the best advice, has evident advantages over private founders in well planning and directing a school; while at the same time his great means and his great influence secure, to a well-planned school of his, credit and authority. This is what, in North Germany, the governors do in the matter of education for the governed; and one may say that they thus give the governed a lesson, and draw out in them the idea of a right reason higher than the suggestions of an ordinary man's ordinary self.[58]

Looking back from the perspective of the present day upon two world cataclysms, the one attributable to the Junker, the other to the Nazi domination, one may realize to some extent how visionary Arnold's doctrine probably was. Mystic and idealistic though it may have been, it was, nevertheless, in its inceptive phase, an outright authoritarianism – a benevolent one, it is true, but one that the British people can be devoutly thankful that they have never over-trusted. Arnold, of course, was expressing a common nineteenth-century doctrine, held notably by Carlyle, whose hero archetype stood as the effectual instrument – an individualized "best self." But besides Carlyle's dour acerbities, Arnold's simple high seriousness takes on the character of moderation. Arnold never manifests the violent passions of Carlyle, whose vindictive reveries envision the immolation of the *canaille* with their reprehensible "swarmeries," and the flogging of the insurgent "niggers" of America and the Indies into a proper humility before their born masters, the heroic, the aristocratic (and, one might add, the megalomaniac) remnant.[59] Arnold's fallacy lurks in a point that he neither overlooks nor ignores, but one that he is willing to accommodate, namely, that the authority of the state must always be vested in men – in an autocrat, a senate, or an elected officialdom – and that this authority must reside at a point remote from the provinces and operate outside the sharp consciousness and

58 *Culture and Anarchy* (Super, v, 154).
59 On Carlyle's affinity with the later Fascist movement, consult Lionel Trilling (p. 54, note). For a statement of Carlyle's theory of the hero as "the best self individualized" and the special appeal his theory had for the Fascists and the Nazis of the twentieth century, see A. C. Taylor, *Carlyle et la Pensée Latine* (Paris, 1937), pp. 376–83. Arnold's differences from, and debts to, Carlyle are treated in detail by David J. DeLaura ("Arnold and Carlyle," *PMLA*, LXXIX (March 1964), 104–29).

effective control of the governed. Its power, moreover, must ultimately rely on force. *"Force till right is ready!"* "The existing order of things!"

But before one may discern the true colour of Arnold's authoritarianism, one must examine his theory of human purpose and personal privilege. For this, one must turn again to "Democracy," his essay prefatory to the *Popular Education of France*.[60] Two principles stand out as essential: one, the native and ineradicable impulse of the human ego toward *expansion*; and two, the organic need of mankind for *equality*. Of the first he says:

Life itself consists, say the philosophers, in the effort *to affirm one's own essence*; meaning by this, to develop one's own existence fully and freely, to have ample light and air, to be neither cramped nor overshadowed. Democracy is trying *to affirm its own essence*; to live, to enjoy, to possess the world, as aristocracy has tried, and successfully tried, before it. ... So potent is the charm of life and expansion upon the living; the moment men are aware of them, they begin to desire them, and the more they have of them, the more they crave.[61]

The second impulse is treated as a corollary of the first:

Now, can it be denied that a certain approach to equality, at any rate a certain reduction of signal inequalities, is a natural, instinctive demand of that impulse which drives society as a whole, – no longer individuals and limited classes only, but the mass of a community, – to develop itself with the utmost possible fulness and freedom? Can it be denied, that to live in a society of equals tends in general to make a man's spirits expand, and his faculties work easily and actively; while, to live in a society of superiors, although it may occasionally be a very good discipline, yet in general tends to tame the spirits and to make the play of the faculties less secure and active? Can it be denied, that to be heavily overshadowed, to be profoundly insignificant, has, on the whole, a depressing and benumbing effect on the character? I know that some individuals react against the strongest impediments, and owe success and greatness to the efforts which they are thus forced to make. But the question is not about individuals. The question is about the common bulk of mankind, persons without extraordinary gifts or exceptional energy, and who will ever

60 Super, II, 3–29. Note especially Super's comments on the Introduction in "Critical and Explanatory Notes," pp. 330–1.
61 *Ibid.*, p. 7.

require, in order to make the best of themselves, encouragement and directly favouring circumstances. Can any one deny, that for these the spectacle, when they would rise, of a condition of splendour, grandeur, and culture, which they cannot possibly reach, has the effect of making them flag in spirit, and of disposing them to sink despondingly back into their own condition? Can any one deny, that the knowledge how poor and insignificant the best condition of improvement and culture attainable by them must be esteemed by a class incomparably richer-endowed, tends to cheapen this modest possible amelioration in the account of those classes also for whom it would be relatively a real progress, and to disenchant their imaginations with it? It seems to me impossible to deny this.[62]

Arnold had none of the intellectual arrogance which so strongly – and tragically – characterized Carlyle. He sought sincerely for leadership within the will of the *demos* – not in the benevolence of some trusted hero. If he chose to rely upon the power of the state as the embodiment of our best selves, he was moved by what he believed to be genuinely democratic motives. He had seen authoritarianism in France and had deprecated there the "excessive action" of the state. He had seen and deplored it in Prussia in the very action of the Minister of Education, who dictated the conditions that should prevail within the schools, even to the conduct and character of the schoolmasters – controlled and obedient men "who will train up their scholars in notions of obedience towards the sovereign and the State." With complete ingenuousness Arnold offered all the evidence:

and I will be candid enough to make bad worse by saying that the present minister, Dr. von Mühler, is what we should call in England, a strong Tory and a strong Evangelical. It is not, indeed, at all likely that in England, with the forces watching and controlling him here, a minister would use language such as I have quoted [namely, that the local people must refrain from all criticism of a candidate for a school post]; and even if it were, I am not at all sure that to have a minister using such language, though it is language which I cordially dislike, is in itself so much more lamentable and baneful a thing than that anarchy and ignorance in educational matters, under which we contentedly suffer.[63]

62 *Ibid.*, pp. 8–9. Lionel Trilling criticizes Arnold for the superficiality of his position and accuses him of political naïveté (pp. 275–91).
63 *Schools and Universities on the Continent* (Super, IV, 228).

Arnold was choosing hopefully between the lesser of two dangers. In urging the reluctant middle class to accept the supremacy of the state, he believed confidently that under the augmenting democratic movements of the day, the cautious beneficiary would discover ample safeguards. The members of the middle class might, in fact, dictate their own conditions and perfect their own creature, that is,

make the condition that this government shall be one of their own adoption, one that they can trust. To ensure this is now in their power. If they do not as yet ensure this, they ought to do so, they have the means of doing so. Two centuries ago they had not; now they have. Having this security, let them now show themselves jealous to keep the action of the State equitable and rational, rather than to exclude the action of the State altogether. If the State acts amiss, let them check it, but let them no longer take it for granted that the State cannot possibly act usefully.[64]

Despite the judgments of his many critics, Arnold probably spoke with some justification. At the heart of the problem is the old question of proportion (not a very dependable principle, it is true, where the exercise of power is concerned). He was but applying in this dilemma of social action some deep-felt semblance of the golden mean: if he were a Frenchman or a Prussian, he would be sternly apprehensive of the encroaching autocratic national government; being an Englishman, he was fearful of the other extreme – the anarchy which results from the frustration of the administrative power.

But before Arnold's position can be vindicated, there is still that one stubborn, enigmatic detail: what is the real nature of that mythopoeic *best self* which is to serve as the animus of the ideal state? He has said to the Philistines that they have nothing to fear, for they themselves can "make the condition that this Government shall be one of their own adoption, one that they can trust." But heretofore he has insisted upon the intellectual qualification, upon the participants' having reached a

64 "Democracy" (Super, II, 26). Arnold's dilemma is expressed well by Ernest Barker: "In the name of good taste or right reason he seeks an authority which will not pander to the bad taste of any class, and which must therefore presumably, be non-representative; and it is difficult to see where such an authority can be found except in a sort of absolute monarchy. Arnold would have instantly denied that he sought anything of this order; he would have treated the idea with elusive and delicate irony; and yet this is the one logical issue of his teaching." (*Political Thought in England from Herbert Spencer to the Present Day*, New York, n. d., p. 199)

cultural majority. He would not establish the provincialism of the Philistines by making their institutions national; he would, rather, delay this nationalization until the benevolent state had disseminated its boon of universal culture and prepared its elect for inspired participation. The blessing was to rain down from above, not to well up from beneath. Actually, then, it would be rule by a remnant, the size of which would gradually increase through the continuing diffusion of sweetness and light.

The remnant! How much of Arnold's concept of authority is comprehended within the restrictive meaning of this term. Late in his life, it became the touchstone for his message to the Americans:

The remnant! – it is the word of the Hebrew prophets also, and especially is it the word of the greatest of them all, Isaiah. Not used with the despondency of Plato, used with far other power informing it, and with a far other future awaiting it, filled with fire, filled with hope, filled with faith, filled with joy, this term itself, *the remnant,* is yet Isaiah's term as well as Plato's. The texts are familiar to all Christendom. "Though thy people Israel be as the sand of the sea, only a remnant of them shall return."[65]

And he offered to the Americans – the expanding millions of a new Philistia – this small deceptive hope: that among the multitudes, *the remnant* might be large enough to speak with an audible voice. For "the majority are unsound."[66]

Arnold's system was, indeed, a benevolent rational authoritarianism, and the promise by which he reassured the Philistines was in fact conditional upon their prior regeneration. In the meantime, the Philistines would not be ousted, but they would be judiciously restrained; not by the aristocracy – and here he rejected the doctrine of Carlyle – not by the

65 "Numbers," *Discourses in America* (*Works,* Ed. de Luxe, IV, 290).

66 Arnold's antipathy to Americans, one that moderated considerably in his later years, seems to be based as much upon his mistrust of majority rule as upon his disgust with the gaucheries of an uncultured electorate. In his *Notebooks* for 1863, he copied this quotation from the *Saturday Review*; but because of the strong Benthamite tinge of this periodical, we should be somewhat cautious in assigning Arnold's true feelings toward it: "The generalities on which the Amern. Decln. of Indence. was grounded, were of English growth; – we do not use such phrases now, because they do not suit us, and they do not suit us because experience shows that they are not true. The experience which shows us that they are not true is that of nearly two generations spent in *practical reforms* of unequalled extent and importance." (*The Note-books of Matthew Arnold,* ed. Lowry, Young, and Dunn, London, 1952, p. 24)

aristocracy, whose young men wishfully "applaud the absolute rulers on the Continent," but by the Levites of culture, men possessed with a harmony of ideas, right reason, and light. The limitation complicated Arnold's position considerably, for the Levites of culture were at best an ineffectual remnant. The government in power is not always benevolent; "the established order of things" is not always dependable nor desirable; it may be – in fact, is – a conflict of "jealous classes, checks, and a dead-lock." And Arnold was himself protesting its present failure.

But to do him justice, it should be pointed out that these earlier judgments were not final, that he stood, even then, in the midst of a philosophical progression toward a more liberal, a more democratic idealism. On 14 December 1867, apropos of the Clerkenwell Prison atrocity, he had had this to say to his mother: "You know I have never wavered in saying that the Hyde Park business eighteen months ago was fatal, and that a Government which dared not deal with a mob, of any nation or with any design, simply opened the flood-gates to anarchy. You cannot have one measure for Fenian rioting and another for English rioting, merely because the design of Fenian rioting is more subversive and desperate; what the State has to do is to put down all rioting with a strong hand, or it is sure to drift into troubles."[67]

Two years later, in *Culture and Anarchy*, his statement was less dogmatic, more tempered with reason:

I mean, it being admitted that the conformity of the individual reason of the fanatical Protestant or the popular rioter with right reason is our object, and not the mere restraining them, by the strong arm of the State, from Papist-baiting, or railing-breaking, – admitting this, we English have so little flexibility that we cannot readily perceive that the State's restraining them from these indulgences may yet fix clearly in their minds that, to the collective nation, these indulgences appear irrational and unallowable, may make them pause and reflect, and may contribute to bringing, with time, their individual reason into harmony with right reason.[68]

There is to be exemplification, then, as well as restraint – the curbing of the violent fanatic, of whatever breed, into a contemplative discovery that there is a better hope – a brooding, benevolent right reason that is both stronger and wiser than he.

But there is still more evidence of a growing tendency toward moderation. In the *Culture and Anarchy* of 1869, and in the earlier *Cornhill*

67 *Letters*, I, 377.   68 Super, v, 160.

version, "Anarchy and Authority,"[69] there appeared a statement of extraordinary violence, a quotation from a letter written by his father, Dr. Thomas Arnold, which he deleted from subsequent editions:

With me, indeed, this rule of conduct is hereditary. I remember my father, in one of his unpublished letters, written more than forty years ago, when the political and social state of the country was gloomy and troubled and there were riots in many places, goes on, after strongly insisting on the badness and foolishness of the government, and on the harm and dangerousness of our feudal and aristocratical constitution of society, and ends thus: "As for rioting, the old Roman way of dealing with that is always the right one; flog the rank and file, and fling the ringleaders from the Tarpeian Rock!"

The excision of this passage from later editions undoubtedly reflects some mellowing of Arnold's earlier convictions – at least of manner.[70] But there is still stronger evidence; for in 1879, eighteen years after the publication of "Democracy," and ten after that of *Culture and Anarchy*, he emphatically repudiated the principle of "benevolent rational absolutism" itself. In his *Mixed Essays*, of which "Democracy" was reprinted as the first, he lifted out the two essential conditions of human uplift, *expansion* and *equality*, and re-enunciated them with telling conviction in a brief preface. It is in this re-statement that the repudiation of absolutism occurs:

Prince Bismarck says: "After all, a benevolent rational absolutism is the best form of government." Plenty of arguments may be adduced in support of such a thesis. The one fatal objection to it is that is is against nature, that it contradicts a vital instinct in man – the instinct of expansion. And a man is not to be civilised or humanised, call it what you will, by thwarting his vital instincts. In fact, the benevolent rational absolu-

69 *Culture and Anarchy: An Essay in Political and Social Criticism* (London, 1869), pp. 196–7; "Anarchy and Authority," *The Cornhill Magazine*, xviii (August 1868), 250. Cf. Trilling, p. 278; and Super, v, "Textual Notes" for pp. 223–7.

70 Apropos of this passage, I have the following comment from Professor Super: "I am probably alone in thinking that Arnold meant this obviously exaggerated statement (as it must have seemed to him) from one of his father's private letters (where, for all we know, it was meant humorously) as fun; and that his deleting it was not a modification of an opinion he never seriously held, but recognition that most people did not see it as a joke."

tism always breaks down. It is found that the ruler cannot in the long run be trusted; it is found that the ruled deteriorate. Why? Because the proceeding is against nature.[71]

But in the earlier years, the years of the essays on education, Arnold had not yet achieved this philosophical position. His attitude then was unmistakably authoritarian, and some may be disposed to ponder the fact a little sadly. He was essentially in conflict with the grossness, the violence, the brutish impetuosity of incipient democracy; in fact, he hated Jacobinism in all its forms. His mystic concept of the state, that apotheosis of our *best self*, might eventually, but not quickly, sublimate the problem. His turning to this distant hope, in fact, blocked the only practical resolution of the conflict: an acceptance of the principle that man learns, finally, by trial and error, by doing and becoming; that in *doing* and *becoming*, more even than in *being*, lies the true satisfaction of his present aspiration, as well as the hope for his expansion.[72] This lesson he might have learned from Mill, whose book, *On Liberty*, he had read.[73] Mill had said that "though individuals may not do the particular thing so well, on the average, as the officers of government, it is nevertheless desirable that it should be done by them, rather than by the government, as a means to their own practical education – a mode of strengthening their active faculties, exercising their judgment, and giving them a familiar knowledge of the subjects with which they are thus left to deal."[74] And for his examples of this salutary exercise of the administrative faculty, Mill pointed to America, where, he said, "let them be left without a government, every body of Americans is able to improvise one, and to carry on that or any other public business with a sufficient amount

71 *Works*, Ed. de Luxe, x, vii.

72 Cp. Hipple, pp. 3–6.

73 On 25 June 1859 he wrote to Mrs. Forster from Strasbourg: "Have you seen Mill's book on Liberty? It is worth reading attentively, being one of the few books that inculcate tolerance in an unalarming and inoffensive way" (*Letters*, I, 96).

74 John Stuart Mill, *On Liberty* (New York, 1929), p. 130. Arnold did, indeed, many years later (1882), utter a similar dictum, but with considerably more reservation than Mill: "It may be better, it is better, that the body of the people, with all its faults, should act for itself, and control its own affairs, than that it should be set aside as ignorant and incapable, and have its affairs managed for it by a so-called superior class, possessing property and intelligence. Property and intelligence cannot be trusted to show a sound majority themselves; the exercise of power by the people tends to educate the people." ("Numbers," *Discourses in America, Works*, Ed. de Luxe, IV, 286)

of intelligence, order, and decision."[75] The function of the state, according to Mill, is to serve as a central reservoir of achieved experience, the active accumulator and diffuser of the best practices, determined after many trials. But to segregate into the department of government the best minds of the land, and to establish these as the professional ruling class of the nation, would, in Mill's opinion, constitute a national hazard, and lead to the atrophy of the powers of public action, as well as to the stagnation of the central bureaucratic authority itself.[76]

The Hyde Park riots of 23 July 1866 serve as an excellent foil for gauging these two contemporary minds. The incident resulted from the defeat of the Gladstone reform bill and the fall of the Liberal government. As a measure of protest over the failure, the Reform League, under the leadership of Edmond Beales, Charles Bradlaugh, Colonel Dickson, and George Holyoake, organized a meeting to be held in Hyde Park, a place then reserved for the exclusive use of the well-to-do. To circumvent this untoward intrusion, the new Home Secretary, Spencer Walpole, ordered the gates of the park to be closed. When the marchers were denied entry, most of them withdrew peaceably to Trafalgar Square, whence they had begun their march. A part of the crowd, however – allegedly under the leadership of Charles Bradlaugh – tore down the railings of the park, resisted the police, overran the flowerbeds, and even threw stones at the houses of the respectable in Belgravia. One wing of the mob evidently also invaded Chester Square, a mile to the south, and smashed the windows in the home of the police commissioner, Sir Richard Mayne – an act of violence actually witnessed with great consternation by the Arnold family.[77]

The disorders certainly aroused in Arnold the apprehension and disgust so characteristic of the genteel classes. His reactions bear the ring of righteous indignation. But they cannot match the smouldering rancour of Carlyle's reckless diatribe:

Nay, have not I a kind of secret satisfaction, of the malicious or even of the judiciary kind (*schadenfreude*, "mischief-joy," the Germans call it, but really it is *justice*-joy withal), that he they call "Dizzy"[78] is to do it;

75 Mill, *On Liberty*, p. 134.
76 *Ibid.*, pp. 134–7. Cf. Frank J. W. Harding, *Matthew Arnold, The Critic, and France* (Genève, 1964), p. 150.
77 Brief accounts of the affair may be found in Trilling, pp. 245–7, and in McCarthy, pp. 100–3.
78 The popular sobriquet of Benjamin Disraeli, author of the successful Reform Bill of August 1867. He became Prime Minister immediately thereafter, hence the object of Carlyle's splenetic glee.

that other jugglers, of an unconscious and deeper type, having sold their poor Mother's body for a mess of Official Pottage, this clever conscious juggler steps in, ... A superlative Hebrew Conjurer, spell-binding all the great Lords, great Parties, great Interests of England, to his hand in this manner, and leading them by the nose, like helpless mesmerised somnambulant cattle, to such issue, – did the world ever see a *flebile ludibrium* of such magnitude before? Lath-sword and Scissors of Destiny; Pickleherring and the Three *Parcae* alike busy in it. This too, I suppose, we had deserved. The end of our poor Old England(such an England as we had at last made of it) to be not a tearful Tragedy, but an ignominious Farce as well! –

Perhaps the consummation may be now nearer than is thought. It seems to me sometimes as if everybody had privately now given-up serious notions of resisting it. Beales and his ragamuffins pull down the railings of Her Majesty's Park, when Her Majesty refuses admittance; Home-Secretary Walpole (representing England's Majesty), listens to a Colonel Dickson talking of "barricades," "improvised pikes," etc.; does *not* order him to be conducted, and if necessary to be kicked, downstairs, with injunction never to return, in case of worse; and when Beales says, "I will see that the Queen's Peace is kept," Queen (by her Walpole) answers, "Will you then; God bless *you!*" and bursts into tears.[79] Those "tears" are certainly an epoch in England; nothing seen, or dreamt of, like them in the History of poor England till now. [80]

It was Mill, the Utilitarian, who intervened judiciously to win deliberation and avert an armed confrontation. The working-class marchers, rebuffed on their first attempt to hold a meeting in Hyde Park, laid plans for another venture to which they proposed to come armed. Walpole prepared to resist them with government troops. It was at this point that Mill, a radical member of Parliament and an avowed friend of labouring men, was invited to a conference with the leaders of the Reform League. He himself recounted the event as follows:

the task fell chiefly upon myself, of persuading them to give up the Hyde Park project, and hold their meeting elsewhere. It was not Mr. Beales

79 The legend of Walpole's weeping on this occasion is apocryphal.
80 "Shooting Niagara: and After?" *Critical and Miscellaneous Essays*, v, 11–12 (Centenary Edition of *The Works of Thomas Carlyle* in Thirty Volumes, New York: Charles Scribner's Sons, 1899, xxx). Carlyle's essay was written in August 1867, the very month of the passage of the Reform Bill and of Disraeli's elevation to the office of Prime Minister.

and Colonel Dickson who needed persuading; on the contrary, it was evident that these gentlemen had already exerted their influence in the same direction, thus far without success. It was the working men who held out, and so bent were they on their original scheme, that I was obliged to have recourse to *les grands moyens*. I told them that a proceeding which would certainly produce a collision with the military, could only be justifiable on two conditions: if the position of affairs had become such that a revolution was desirable, and if they thought themselves able to accomplish one. To this argument, after considerable discussion, they at last yielded; and I was able to inform Mr. Walpole that their intention was given up. I shall never forget the depth of his relief or the warmth of his expressions of gratitude.[81]

One of the principals in the Hyde Park riot, Charles Bradlaugh, serves also to reflect the contrast between Arnold's attitudes and those of Mill. Apparently it was Bradlaugh's wing of the Reform League marchers who refused to withdraw when confronted by the police; it was they who broke down the palings and trampled the gardens. Throughout *Culture and Anarchy* and *Friendship's Garland*, Bradlaugh stands in Arnold's mind as a *bête noire* of violence and mob rule.[82] He represents "the excess of the working class ... who seems to be almost for baptising us all in blood and fire into his new social dispensation. ... Mr. Bradlaugh, like our types of excess in the aristocratic and middle classes, is evidently capable, if he had his head given him, of running us all into great dangers and confusion."[83]

Mill, on the other hand, had risked and suffered the displeasure of both the Tory and the Liberal parties by subscribing to the election expenses of Bradlaugh – a measure of support he (Mill) steadfastly refused to provide in his own behalf. "I knew him to be a man of ability," Mill said, "and he had proved that he was the reverse of a demagogue, ..." Mill, of course, had strong affective bonds with the labouring classes, whom Bradlaugh represented. It was men of this sort, he felt, who "were needed, as it seemed to me, in Parliament, and I did not think that Mr. Bradlaugh's anti-religious opinions (even though he had been intem-

81 *The Autobiography of John Stuart Mill* (New York, 1944), pp. 203–4.
82 George Odger, by way of contrast, invariably symbolizes for Arnold "the beautiful and virtuous mean of our present working class," although he also has, "manifestly, with all his good points, some insufficiency of light" (Super, v, 133 and note to 133: 20 on pp. 430–1).
83 *Ibid.*

perate in the expression of them) ought to exclude him."[84] Arnold, certainly, could never have concurred with the latter judgment, he whose nature yearned after the comforts of the Establishment. Mill believed in pragmatic reason, and he sought its cultivation through the participation of the people in the affairs which most concerned them. This was his earnest lesson for the leaders of the new democracy.

Arnold did not learn this lesson quickly, although he had accepted and expressed some of its constituent tenets; immediate chaos was too abhorrent to his refined and sensitive nature. The spirit of licence was foreign to his temperament – to his faith in the beneficent reign of "right reason and the will of God."' And many of the devotees of culture will be eager to believe with him, and to shelter under the strength and beauty of his vindication.

It was Carlyle who, in speaking of his poet hero, Dante, cited Coleridge's pertinent remark: "that wherever you find a sentence musically worded, of true rhythm and melody in the words, there is something deep and good in the meaning too. For body and soul, word and idea, go strangely together here as elsewhere."[85] What a fitting comment on the serene high-seriousness of *Culture and Anarchy* and the earlier "Democracy." Truly they shadow forth something of the universal verity. But if one will turn resolutely away from delectation and flagellate his enchanted wits, he may perceive about the prophet's head – within these middle years, at least – the faint, the almost imperceptible aura of the ineffectual angel.

It is in the building of speculative systems that the wraith of imperfection lurks, and with Arnold it is in the realm of theory that we find the broken arcs; beneath the philosophical superstructure, there is yet a perfect round – Arnold's maturing concept of a national institution of public education, the as-yet-unformed instrument of England's potential greatness. With the development of that concept, the genesis of *Culture and Anarchy* is congruent. Its outlines had appeared to Arnold during his mission to the continent in 1859, and all of them had been expressed some years before the publication of the great definitive essay itself: in *England and the Italian Question,* in the official report to the Newcastle Commission, in "Democracy," and in *A French Eton.*

84 *Autobiography*, pp. 219–20.
85 *Heroes and Hero-Worship* (Centenary Edition of *The Works of Thomas Carlyle* in Thirty Volumes, v), p. 90.

V

Conclusion

A benevolent rational authoritarianism is against nature, Arnold said. If this is true, a corollary seems clear and definite: man bears within his nature the need for freedom, the craving for the amplitude to become. It follows, also, that the lines of democratic advancement are then inevitable, for nature itself impels them. Surely Arnold moved ever forward along these lines, impelled, it would appear, by a vigorous innate humanism.

But Arnold, like all other men, attained his stature gradually. The youthful exuberances of the letters to Clough bear yet the taint of Carlylean arrogance later to be erased; the inspired exposition of the powers of *expansion* and *equality* in "Democracy" were tempered by a cautious – perhaps subconscious – craving for restraint. "Now, and for us," he said in the preface to *Culture and Anarchy*, "it is a time to Hellenise, and to praise knowing; for we have Hebraised too much, and have overvalued doing."[1] These facts should certainly remind us that the lessons of democracy come slowly. They are not learned within the span of a single generation, nor are they comprehended often within the compass of one man's mind.

Among the seers of the century, Mill probably stands as the most advanced in his dialectic. *On Liberty* comes close to the standard of faultless texts. Philosophically, Mill holds a pragmatic position, whereas Arnold clings temperamentally to the old Platonic cast of thought. And there is no escaping the authoritarian ring of the latter position; though the king may be a true philosopher, out of his questionable vision he must govern lesser men. Arnold, indeed, would eventually supplant him with a broadening electorate – a slowly expanding remnant redeemed through the power of sweetness and light.

Despite Arnold's temperamental caution in these matters, the tenor of

1 Super, v, 255.

his life was lofty, and his students are drawn inevitably into a higher orbit of thought. "High seriousness," "sweetness and light" – these are not idle epithets. Their essence pervades the essays as it does the poems. Indeed, it tends to enchant the reader into a growing harmonic conviction, and he discovers that the fences of disinterest require a constant mending. There is great dignity, too, in Arnold's steadfast resolution, in his firm determination not to shirk his desolating duties. Upon his retiring from the inspectorship in 1886, the teachers of his district honoured him and Mrs. Arnold with a dinner and a handsome present. In his pungent and eloquent response, he indulged in a reminiscence of the the manner in which he had managed to bear his burden:

Though I am a schoolmaster's son I confess that school teaching or school inspecting is not the line of life I should naturally have chosen. I adopted it in order to marry a lady who is here to-night, and who feels the kindness as warmly and gratefully as I do. (Cheers.) My wife and I had a wandering life of it at first. There were but three inspectors for all England. My district went right across from Pembroke Dock to Great Yarmouth. We had no home; one of our children was born in a lodging at Derby, with a workhouse, if I recollect right, behind and a penitentiary in front. (Laughter.) But the irksomeness of my new duties was what I felt most, and during the first year or so this was sometimes almost insupportable. But I met daily in the schools with men and women discharging duties akin to mine, duties as irksome as mine, duties less well paid than mine, and I asked myself, Are they on roses? Would not they by nature prefer, many of them, to go where they liked and do what they liked, instead of being shut up in a school? I saw them making the best of it; I saw the cheerfulness and efficiency with which they did their work, and I asked myself again, How do they do it? Gradually it grew into a habit with me to put myself into their places, to try and enter into their feelings, to represent to myself their life, and I assure you I got many lessons from them. This placed me in sympathy with them. Seeing people once a year is not much, but when you have come into sympathy with them they do not fade from your mind, and I find myself able to recall, and almost daily recalling, names and faces and circumstances of teachers whom I have not seen for years. That is because I have been in sympathy with them. I will not accept all the praise you have given me, but I will accept this – I have been fair and I have been sympathetic. (Cheers.)[2]

2 The entire speech appeared the next morning in the (London) *Times*, No.

The Education Act of 1870 did away with denominational inspection and led to a much more convenient organization of the inspectorial districts. At this time Arnold was assigned the compact district of Westminster in London and the outlying suburban district of Edmonton. He was also given the services of an assistant inspector, Thomas Healing, who undoubtedly relieved him of much drudgery. Healing has recorded many significant comments on Arnold's relationship with teachers, managers, and members of the official staff. "I was struck," said Healing, "by his perfect frankness and candour in all his educational relationships. He never pretended to be an oracle in methods of instruction, and therefore never attempted to prescribe to teachers the precise methods they were to use, though he would often kindly criticise a teacher's mode of handling a subject if it lacked simplicity or breadth of treatment."[3]

Healing also confirmed the constructive and liberalizing influence which Arnold exerted upon the schools that he inspected. He was always ready to praise originality of treatment, said Healing, and to allow the teacher "full liberty to give any turn to the instruction for which his special tastes and acquirements qualified him." Always concerned over the want of general culture in the pupil-teachers and in the students in the training colleges, he constantly encouraged the inclusion in their studies of the formative matters – portions of the best English authors and composition. He also encouraged higher education for teachers, often inducing a young teacher to matriculate at the University of London in the effort to qualify eventually for a degree. "If he found a young man of promise in a school," said Healing, "he generally had with him some serious and sympathetic talk on this subject; and some have told me in the after years that they would never have attempted a work of such difficulty but for the stimulus applied by Mr. Arnold."[4]

Having once entered the toils, it was Arnold's mission to move within the grey world of school inspection as a bearer of light – perhaps unconscious of his exemplary role. Sir Joshua Fitch relates the comments of the Very Rev. George D. Boyle, the Dean of Salisbury,[5] concerning "the intense refreshment and pleasure he had when Matthew Arnold came to inspect a school at Kidderminster."

31,916 (13 November 1886), p. 5. Reprinted in Neiman, *Essays, Letters, and Reviews*, pp. 306–10.

3 Fitch, p. 173.

4 *Ibid.*, pp. 173–4.

5 The Very Rev. George David Boyle, Curate of Kidderminster from 1853 to 1857; Vicar of Kidderminster in 1867; appointed Dean of Salisbury in 1880 (*Dictionary of National Biography*, Second Supplement).

"I once," he [Dean Boyle] adds, "heard a famous preacher at Oxford compare a student's first acquaintance with Bengel's *Commentary* to the admission of a ray of light when a shutter was opened in a darkened room. The arrival of Matthew Arnold at my lodging was something like this. He brought with him a complete atmosphere of culture and poetry. He had something to tell of Sainte-Beuve's last criticism, some new book like Lewes' *Life of Goethe* to recommend, some new political interest to unfold, and, in short, he carried you away from the routine of every-day life with his enthusiasm and his spirit. He gave me most valuable advice as to the training of pupil-teachers. 'Open their minds,' he would say, 'take them into the world of Shakespeare, and try to make them feel that there is no book so full of poetry and beauty as the Bible.' He had something to tell me of Stanley and Clough, and it is really difficult to say what a delightful tonic effect his visits produced. ... One of his pleasantest characteristics was his perfect readiness to discuss with complete command of temper, views and opinions of his own which he knew I did not share and thought dangerous. All who knew him constantly regretted that a man of such wonderful gifts should have to spend his life in the laborious duties of a School Inspector."[6]

Occasionally the anecdotes fall into the humorous vein. One young inspector, Edmund Mackenzie Sneyd-Kynnersley, numbers Arnold among the "two or three Inspectors of Schools who were more distinguished than any whom I have known in later years," and he accords to Arnold the role of supplying the office with amusement.

Arnold's district consisted of Westminster and Edmonton, a ridiculous grouping. ... By the Treasury rules, if his work at Edmonton required his attendance for two or more consecutive days, he was bound after the first day to spend the night there, or to refrain from charging his train and cab fares home again. Being a poet, of course he returned home, and charged his fare every day. "The knight of the Blue Pencil," as he called his enemy, sharpened his blue pencil, and wrote – "Mr. M. Arnold, H.M.I. Why not stay at Edmonton?" And the great man plaintively replied: "How can you expect me to stay at Edmonton, when John Gilpin couldn't?" The account was passed.[7]

But as Dean Boyle suggested, it would be difficult to name a person with more positive, well-ordered convictions, and with more consistency in

6 Fitch, pp. 167–8.
7 *H. M. I. Passages in the Life of an Inspector of Schools* (London: The Macmillan Co., 1908), p. 198.

the dominant tenor of his voluminous works, both official and literary. Even in practical matters, Arnold spoke always with a well-grounded understanding of the critical function – the need to control one's whims and prepossessions, the duty to consider all sides of a question, the responsibility to maintain a stoical indifference as to consequences, to say what the cold, dispassionate judgment dictates and let the conclusions strike where they may. It was this stern, unbending critical temper that caused him to excoriate the Nonconformists, to criticize the formalized preoccupations of the public schools, to arraign the universities for their lassitude and disregard of science, to castigate the Liberal party for its confused and shapeless policy. At the fall of the Gladstone Ministry in 1874, he wrote to his sister "K," whose husband had just stepped down: "I do not affect to be sorry at the change; the Liberal party, it seemed to me, had no body of just, clear, well-ordered thought upon politics, and were only superior to the Conservative in not having for their rule of conduct merely the negative instinct against change; now they will have to examine their minds and find what they really want and mean to try for."[8]

Here is reflected faithfully the disinterested temper of Arnold's critical mind. And it was this quality that pervaded his professional reports. The quality of these reports is wonderfully impressive, as is also the persistence with which British governmental officials besought his services for the several royal commissions. No doubt there was a direct relationship between the clarity and the cogency of the reports, and the frequency of his reappointments. It is evident, in fact, that Arnold came to enjoy a cumulative prestige amounting to an oracular authority. A year after his retirement from the inspectorship, he sat for two full days before the Cross Commissioners, submitting to a cross-questioning on his many observations of foreign schools and his opinions on the comparable practices of his own country.[9] Writing to Mrs. Arnold, who was then in America visiting their daughter,[10] he said of this ordeal: "I got on well enough in my examination, but I find I have made, having to answer questions suddenly, mistakes on points of fact which I never should make in writing a report, when I go to my documents for all I say, and even write to my foreign informants if I am in doubt; however, I hope to correct my evidence before it circulates."[11]

8 *Letters*, II, 112 (February 1874).
9 *First Report of the Royal Commissioners*, pp. 184–225.
10 Married to Frederick W. Whitridge of New York.
11 *Letters*, II, 329 (April 24, 1886).

Many were the references, by Arnold's interlocutors during this inquisition, to the substance of the foreign reports; and this is evidence enough that British officials at least had read and pondered them. Archer comments upon the scope of his influence as follows:

His educational views were the direct outcome of his attitude as a prophet, and they can be read in the present age with approval. But they were in advance of his time and, though what he wrote was highly valued by Royal Commissions and by educational reformers, as far as immediate effect on educational legislation and administration was concerned he was a voice crying in the wilderness. What better proof can we have that educational advance is due to the efforts of individuals than this instance of the State appointing a man of genius as one of its educational officials and then finding that he re-shaped educational ideas during his leisure hours devoted to literary criticism, while his official work largely consisted in effectively denouncing the policy of his superiors![12]

This, it seems, is a fair judgment; and while it leaves the scope of Arnold's service nebulously outlined, it implies a truth that can scarcely be questioned, that his influence was both vast and wise.

As for the consistency of his thought, it is all comprehended within his one great dream for humanity. "The aim for all of us," he said, "is to make civilisation pervasive and general"; but amid the chaos and confusion of his time, the consummation seemed often to be very far away. "Undoubtedly, that aim is not given by the life which we now see around us," he said. "Undoubtedly, it is given by 'a sentiment of the ideal life.' But then the ideal life is, in sober and practical truth, 'none other than man's normal life, as we shall one day know it.' "[13]

Here is the essence of his unifying principle, as well as the epitome of his plan. It was enunciated in his "Democracy," and it ramifies throughout the whole body of his critical, literary, and educational works: to secure "a more deliberate and systematically reasoned action on the part of the State in dealing with education in this country"; to organize and mobilize the state, as the embodiment of our best selves; to demand of it a worthy initiative, a standard of rational and equitable action; to invoke its admirable genius, "greater than the genius of any individual, greater

12 Richard Laurence Archer, *Secondary Education in the Nineteenth Century* (Cambridge, 1928), p. 185.
13 *Mixed Essays* (*Works*, Ed. de Luxe, x, ix).

even than Shakespeare's genius, for it includes the genius of Newton also."

The tenacity with which he clung to this principle led him sometimes into questionable and dogmatic choices. For example, it impelled him to oppose the Burials Bill of 1876, which would have granted to Dissenting ministers the right to conduct burial services in the churchyard for members of their own congregations. Denied this privilege by British law, Dissenters had been compelled to seek the good offices of clergymen of the Establishment, who were not in all cases either generous enough or easy enough in conscience to comply. Arnold, indeed, urged that they should comply. But to open the churchyard, a public place, to "the observances of ignorant and fanatical little sects" to parade themselves without taste and without dignity before the public eye, offended his good sense. "Speech-making and prayer-making, substitutions or additions of individual invention, hazarded *ex tempore*," he said, "seem to me unsuitable and undesirable for such a place and such an occasion."[14] It is the difference between a reading from Milton and one from Eliza Cook.[15] "Taking man in his totality and in the long run, bad music and bad poetry, to whatever good and useful purposes a man may often manage to turn them, are in themselves mischievous and deteriorating to him. Somewhere and somehow, and at some time or other, he has to pay a penalty and to suffer a loss for taking delight in them."[16]

Even where he treads close upon the brink of error, Arnold is impelled by motives that are good; and if he has his foibles, surely they shrink to insignificance against the great monument of his work and the great example of his life. "The great monument of his work"? This brings us to the weighing of another inevitability: the cost of the poet's sacrifice! Arnold's poetry represents – some titles to the contrary – an early epoch in his busy life. The period of his high poetic production corresponds roughly with the years preceding and including his first decade as an inspector of schools. His volume, *New Poems*, of 1867 contains, it is true, a substantial body of new work – thirty-nine titles, in fact – combined with seven older ones. But later volumes represent for the most part revisions and rearrangements of earlier contents, with a few additions of still later things. Clearly, Arnold's poetry suffered a gradual, then a more precipitate displacement by the encroaching pressures of his public

14 "A Last Word on the Burials Bill," *Last Essays on Church and Religion* (*Works*, Ed. de Luxe, IX, 408).

15 "Irish Catholicism and British Liberalism," *Mixed Essays* (*Works*, Ed. de Luxe, X, 133).

16 "A Last Word on the Burials Bill," p. 409.

career. The eclipse of the earlier interest was not effected without some frustration. There are nostalgic comments in the *Letters* that betray the conflict which the relinquishment of the poetic life entailed. There is, moveover, an affinity of tone between the poems and the letters written during the first sombre decade of Arnold's official career. Both, indeed, distill the mournful spirit of the "Stanzas from the Grande Chartreuse," of one who is hopelessly

> *Wandering between two worlds, one dead,*
> *The other powerless to be born,*
> *With nowhere yet to rest my head,*
> *Like these, on earth I wait forlorn.*
> *Their faith, my tears, the world deride –*
> *I come to shed them at their side.*

The facts are that the years of Arnold's inspectorship up to 1859 represent a great spiritual climacteric of his life, characterized by frustration, sadness, and unrest, as the tones of his poetry attest; that his official journey to the Continent marked the end of this dark interval and the moment of a great spiritual rebirth; that in stepping on the soil of France, he beheld at once the larger vision of his own calling as a servant of the benevolent and enlightened state in disseminating culture – a knowledge of right reason and the will of God – among a grateful people.

From this moment onward the course of Arnold's critical thought was forced more and more into the educational vein. The poet began to give place to the essayist, the creator of *belles lettres* to the commentator on practical affairs. One is inclined to wonder whether the transformation might not have been even more pronounced had it not been for one restraining circumstance – his ten-year incumbency of the Poetry Chair at Oxford, to which he had been elected in May of 1857. His election to this honour certainly commanded his purely literary work, resulting in the writing of *Merope* (1858), *On Translating Homer* (1861), *On the Study of Celtic Literature* (1867), and a long series of critical essays later collected in *Essays in Criticism* (First Series). There is, then, this literary strand of Arnold's work which persisted throughout his life and culminated in the "Milton" and the "Shelley" of his last year (1888).

But with the *England and the Italian Question* of 1859, Arnold initiated another line of endeavour, the constructive criticism of current affairs – politics, education, and religion – the regeneration, in fact, of man in his society. In this phase of his work, it is the educational factor that emerges as the focus of his thought; all things gravitate to this prime centre – the dissemination of a broad culture through the intervention of the ideal state, that embodiment of the best selves of an enlightened people. The theme reaches its climax, or at least its most eloquent expression in the *Culture and Anarchy* of 1869; but its dominant strains were sounded earlier – in *England and the Italian Question,* in *The Popular Education of France,* in "Democracy," and in *A French Eton,* all written during the first flush of the new enthusiasm, imparted by the invigorating air of France.

The common approach to a study of Arnold has been, naturally, through the *belles lettristic* works – through the poetry, the prefaces, and the critical essays. Herein lies another testimony to the credo he so eloquently upheld – the immense power of letters in human life. But it would be an error to seek within this centre the dominant effort of his life. Although his interest in humane letters began earlier and persisted to the end, it soon became overshadowed by and finally absorbed into the mightier stream; the labour begun in drudgery became the grand mission.

It is a mistake, therefore, to neglect Arnold's official side. The heart of his doctrine may be found, it is true, in the old familiar places, but not the background. No man's thought is rooted deeper in current affairs. In the worker and the teacher, the soul of Arnold is to be surprised. From the homely soil of the democratic struggle, from its conflict and confusion, his ideas were brought to flower. His life serves well to remind us that "In the sounding labour-house vast Of being," there are values never to be fully known or reckoned. There is a fine unconscious self-commentary in what he said of Wordsworth in "The Youth of Nature":

> *Well may we mourn, when the head*
> *Of a sacred poet lies low*
> *In an age which can rear them no more!*
> *The complaining millions of men*
> *Darken in labour and pain;*
> *But he was a priest to us all*
> *Of the wonder and bloom of the world,*
> *Which we saw with his eyes, and were glad.*

There is another commentary on his life which emanates from the intimate heart of the family – the excerpts from his notebooks gathered after his death by his wife and daughter. Here we may read and ponder another fair vision – a good man collecting and preserving for continued reflection the best thoughts of others – thoughts gathered from many distant sources and written in six different languages, ancient and modern:

Il faut que les esprits soient satisfaits et s'élèvent en même temp que les intérêts se sentent garantis et se confient.

[Guizot, *Mémoires pour servir à l'histoire de mon temps,* iv. 284.]

Gerson said: The reformation of the Church must have its beginning among the young children. In a letter to the students of the College of Navarre, written from Bruges he says: Credendum est quod in tantâ angustiâ temporis, et inter tot animarum pericula non multùm placebit ludere, ne dicam phantasiari, circa ea quæ prorsus supervacua sunt.

["Rememoratio," *Opera Omnia,* ii. 109; "Duæ Epistolæ ... de Reformatione Theologiæ," *Opera Omnia,* i. 124.]

Il faut tâcher d'être bon, d'adoucir son caractère, de calmer ses passions, de posséder son âme, d'écarter les haines injustes, d'attendrir son humeur autant que cela est en nous, et, quand on ne le peut pas, de sauver du moins son esprit du désordre de son cœur, d'affranchir ses jugements de la tyrannie des passions. Vauvenargues (died at 37).

[Vauvenargues, quoted in Sainte-Beuve, *Causeries du lundi,* xiv. 50.]

n'aspirant qu'à être étendu et conciliant!

[Sainte-Beuve, 'Vauvenargues,' ibid. 53.]

Le laisser-aller est dangereux dans le bonheur: il l'est bien plus dans le malheur. Quand je suis malheureux, je tire l'épée de son fourreau et je combats ma peine à outrance. Bonstetten (died at 86).

[Bonstetten, quoted in Sainte-Beuve, *Causeries du lundi,* xiv. 474][17]

His daughter remarks on the "deep unconscious significance" of the entry chosen for Sunday, 15 April 1888, the last day of his life: "Weep bitterly over the dead, as he is worthy, and then comfort thyself; drive heaviness away: thou shalt not do him good but hurt thyself" *Ecclesiast-icus,* xxxviii.[18]

17 The transcription of the most edifying quotations from the miscellaneous jottings in Arnold's notebooks was begun by Mrs. Arnold and was completed after her death by their daughter, Eleanor Wodehouse, Viscountess Sandhurst (*Matthew Arnold's Notebooks,* London: Smith, Elder & Co., 1902). In 1928, upon the discovery of seventeen of the missing notebooks, Howard Foster Lowry, Karl Young, and Waldo Hilary Dunn began a twenty-year research into the sources of the literary items. The result was an invaluable book: *The Note-books of Matthew Arnold* (London, New York, Toronto, 1952). The quotations were taken from the latter text, pp. 13–14.

18 *Matthew Arnold's Notebooks,* ed. Eleanor Wodehouse (London, 1902), p. viii.

BIBLIOGRAPHY

ADAMS, FRANCIS. *History of the Elementary School Contest in England.* London: Chapman and Hall, Ltd., 1882.

ALEXANDER, EDWARD. *Matthew Arnold and John Stuart Mill.* New York: Columbia University Press, 1965.

ARCHER, RICHARD LAURENCE. *Secondary Education in the Nineteenth Century.* Cambridge: The University Press, 1928.

ARMYTAGE, W.H.G. "George Odger (1820–1877): A Founder of the British Labour Movement." *University of Toronto Quarterly* XVIII (October 1948): 68–75.

———— "Matthew Arnold and Richard Cobden in 1864: Some Recently Discovered Letters." *Review of English Studies* XXV (July 1949): 249–54.

———— "Matthew Arnold and T. H. Huxley: Some New Letters, 1870–1880." *Review of English Studies* IV, n.s. (1953): 346–53.

———— "Matthew Arnold and W. E. Gladstone: Some New Letters." *University of Toronto Quarterly* XVIII (April 1949), 217–26.

ARNOLD, MATTHEW. *The Complete Prose Works of Matthew Arnold.* Edited by Robert H. Super. Ann Arbor: The University of Michigan Press, 1960–5. 5 vols. (Referred to in text as Super. Individual works listed alphabetically below.)

———— *The Complete Works of Matthew Arnold,* Ed. de Luxe. London: Macmillan and Co., Ltd., 1903–4. 11 vols. (Referred to in text as *Works,* Ed. de Luxe. Individual works listed alphabetically below.)

———— "Anarchy and Authority." *The Cornhill Magazine* XVII (January 1868): 30–47; XVII (February 1868): 239–56; XVIII (August 1868): 239–56.

———— "The Church of England." In *Last Essays on Church and Religion (The Complete Works of Matthew Arnold,* Ed. de Luxe. Vol. IX. London: Macmillan and Co., Ltd., 1903–4).

——— *Civilization in the United States, First and Last Impressions of America.* Boston: Cupples and Hurd, 1888.

——— "The Code out of Danger" (*The Complete Prose Works of Matthew Arnold.* Edited by Robert H. Super. Vol. II. Ann Arbor: The University of Michigan Press, 1962).

——— *Culture and Anarchy* (*The Complete Prose Works of Matthew Arnold.* Edited by Robert H. Super. Vol. V. Ann Arbor: The University of Michigan Press, 1965).

——— *Culture and Anarchy: An Essay in Political and Social Criticism.* London: Smith, Elder, and Co., 1869.

——— "Culture and Its Enemies." *The Cornhill Magazine* XVI (July 1867): 36–53.

——— "Ecce, Convertimur ad Gentes." *Fortnightly Review* XXV, n.s. (1 February 1879), 238–52; republished in *Irish Essays*, 1882 (*The Complete Works of Matthew Arnold*, Ed. de Luxe. Vol. XI. London: Macmillan and Co., Ltd., 1903–4).

——— *England and the Italian Question* (*The Complete Prose Works of Matthew Arnold.* Edited by Robert H. Super. Vol. I. Ann Arbor: The University of Michigan Press, 1960).

——— "Farewell speech at a dinner given by the teachers of Westminster upon the occasion of Arnold's resignation as Inspector of Schools." The (London) *Times*, no. 31,916 (13 November 1886; reprinted in Fraser Neiman, *Essays, Letters, and Reviews by Matthew Arnold.* Cambridge: Harvard University Press, 1960, pp. 306–11).

——— *A French Eton* (*The Complete Prose Works of Matthew Arnold.* Edited by Robert H. Super. Vol. II. Ann Arbor: The University of Michigan Press, 1962).

——— *Friendship's Garland* (*The Complete Prose Works of Matthew Arnold.* Edited by Robert H. Super. Vol. V. Ann Arbor: The University of Michigan Press, 1965).

——— "The Function of Criticism at the Present Time" (*The Complete Prose Works of Matthew Arnold.* Edited by Robert H. Super. Vol. III. Ann Arbor: The University of Michigan Press, 1962).

——— *God and the Bible* (*The Complete Works of Matthew Arnold*, Ed. de Luxe. Vol. VIII. London: Macmillan and Co., Ltd., 1903–4).

——— "A Guide to English Literature." In *Mixed Essays* (*The Complete Works of Matthew Arnold*, Ed. de Luxe. Vol. X. London: Macmillan and Co., Ltd., 1903–4).

——— *A Guide to English Literature* and *Essay on Gray* (with *On the Study of Literature* by John Morley). New York: Macmillan and Co., 1896.

——— "The Incompatibles." In *Irish Essays, and Others* (*The Complete Works of Matthew Arnold*, Ed. de Luxe. Vol. XI. London: Macmillan and Co., Ltd., 1903–4).

——— "Irish Catholicism and British Liberalism." In *Mixed Essays* (*The Complete Works of Matthew Arnold*, Ed. de Luxe. Vol. x. London: Macmillan and Co., Ltd., 1903–4).

——— *Isaiah* xl–lxvi, with the shorter prophecies allíed to it, arranged and edited with notes by Matthew Arnold. London: Macmillan and Co., 1875.

——— "A Last Word on the Burials Bill." In *Last Essays on Church and Religion* (*The Complete Works of Matthew Arnold*, Ed. de Luxe. Vol. ix. London: Macmillan and Co., Ltd., 1903–4).

——— *Letters of Matthew Arnold, 1848–1888.* Edited by George W. E. Russell. 2 vols. London: Macmillan and Co., 1895.

——— *Literature and Dogma* (*The Complete Prose Works of Matthew Arnold.* Edited by Robert H. Super. Vol. vi. Ann Arbor: The University of Michigan Press, 1968).

——— *Matthew Arnold's Notebooks, and a Portrait.* Edited by Eleanor Wodehouse (Viscountess Sandhurst). London: Smith, Elder, and Co., 1902.

——— "Maurice de Guérin" (*The Complete Prose Works of Matthew Arnold.* Edited by Robert H. Super. Vol. iii. Ann Arbor: The University of Michigan Press, 1962).

——— "Mr. Walter and Schoolmasters' Certificates" (*The Complete Prose Works of Matthew Arnold.* Edited by Robert H. Super. Vol. ii. Ann Arbor: The University of Michigan Press, 1962).

——— *The Note-books of Matthew Arnold.* Edited by Howard Foster Lowry, Karl Young, and Waldo Hilary Dunn. London, New York and Toronto: Oxford University Press, 1952.

——— "Numbers." In *Discourses in America* (*The Complete Works of Matthew Arnold*, Ed. de Luxe. Vol. iv. London: Macmillan and Co., Ltd., 1903–4).

——— "On the Modern Element in Literature" (*The Complete Prose Works of Matthew Arnold.* Edited by Robert H. Super. Vol. i. Ann Arbor: The University of Michigan Press, 1960).

——— "On Translating Homer: Last Words" (*The Complete Prose Works of Matthew Arnold.* Edited by Robert H. Super. Vol. i. Ann Arbor: The University of Michigan Press, 1960).

——— *The Poems of Matthew Arnold, 1840–1867.* Introduction by Sir Arthur T. Quiller-Couch. London: Oxford University Press, 1930.

——— *The Popular Education of France, with Notices of That of Holland and Switzerland* (*The Complete Prose Works of Matthew Arnold.* Edited by Robert H. Super. Vol ii. Ann Arbor: The University of Michigan Press, 1962).

——— "Preface." In *Mixed Essays* (*The Complete Works of Matthew Arnold*, Ed. de Luxe. Vol. x. London: Macmillan and Co., Ltd., 1903–4).

———— "The Principle of Examination" (*The Complete Prose Works of Matthew Arnold*. Edited by Robert H. Super. Vol. II. Ann Arbor: The University of Michigan Press, 1962).

———— *Reports on Elementary Schools, 1852–1882.* Edited by Sir Francis Sandford. London: Macmillan and Co., 1889.

———— *St. Paul and Protestantism* (*The Complete Prose Works of Matthew Arnold*. Edited by Robert H. Super. Vol. VI. Ann Arbor: The University of Michigan Press, 1968).

———— "Sainte-Beuve" (*The Complete Prose Works of Matthew Arnold*. Edited By Robert H. Super. Vol. V. Ann Arbor: The University of Michigan Press, 1965).

———— "Schools" (*The Reign of Queen Victoria*. Edited by Thomas Humphry Ward. Vol. II. London: Smith, Elder, and Co., 1887).

———— *Schools and Universities on the Continent* (*The Complete Prose Works of Matthew Arnold*. Edited by Robert H. Super. Vol. IV. Ann Arbor: The University of Michigan Press, 1964).

———— *Special Report on Certain Points Connected with Elementary Education in Germany, Switzerland, and France.* Great Britain, Parliament. House of Commons, Command Paper 4752. Vol. LI. London: Eyre and Spottiswoode, 1886. (Reprinted by the Education Reform League. London: Toynbee Hall, Whitechapel, E., 1888.)

———— "The Twice-Revised Code." *Fraser's Magazine* LXV (March 1862): 347–65 (*The Complete Prose Works of Matthew Arnold*. Edited by Robert H. Super. Vol. II. Ann Arbor: The University of Michigan Press, 1962).

———— *The Unpublished Letters of Matthew Arnold.* Edited by Arnold Whitridge. New Haven: Yale University Press, 1923.

BAINES, EDWARD. "Lord John Russell's Plan of Education." The (London) *Times* CCCXXIX, no. 22 (31 March 1856): 12.

BAMFORD, THOMAS WILLIAM. *Thomas Arnold.* London: Cresset Press, 1960.

BARKER, ERNEST. *Political Thought in England from Herbert Spencer to the Present Day.* New York: H. Holt and Co., 1915?

BEVINGTON, MERLE M. *Matthew Arnold's England and the Italian Question.* Durham: Duke University Press, 1953.

BIBBY, CYRIL. *T. H. Huxley, Scientist, Humanist, and Educator.* New York: Horizon Press, 1960.

BINNS, HENRY BRYAN. *A Century of Education, Being the Centenary History of the British and Foreign School Society, 1808–1908.* London: J. M. Dent and Co., 1908.

BONNEROT, LOUIS. *Matthew Arnold, Poète.* Paris: M. Didier, 1947.

BUCKLER, WILLIAM E. *Matthew Arnold's Books; toward a Publishing Diary.* Genève: E. Droz, 1958.

BURKE, EDMUND. *Letters, Speeches, and Tracts on Irish Affairs.*

Collected and arranged by Matthew Arnold. London: Macmillan and Co., 1881.

CARLYLE, THOMAS. *Heroes and Hero Worship* (The Centenary Edition of *The Works of Thomas Carlyle* in Thirty Volumes. Vol. v. New York: Charles Scribner's Sons, 1899).

———— "Shooting Niagara: and After?" In *Critical and Miscellaneous Essays*, Vol. v (The Centenary Edition of *The Works of Thomas Carlyle* in Thirty Volumes. Vol. xxx. New York: Charles Scribner's Sons, 1899).

COLERIDGE, ERNEST HARTLEY. *Life and Correspondence of John Duke Lord Coleridge*. London: W. Heinemann, 1904.

CONNELL, WILLIAM FRASER. *The Educational Thought and Influence of Matthew Arnold*. London: Routledge and K. Paul, 1950.

CRAIK, SIR HENRY. *The State in Its Relation to Education*. London: Macmillan and Co., 1884.

DELAURA, DAVID J. "Arnold and Carlyle." *PMLA* LXXIX (March 1964): 104–29.

"Educational Movements." *Westminster Review* LIV (January 1851): 196–210.

First Report of the Royal Commissioners Appointed to Inquire into the Working of the Elementary Education Acts, England and Wales. London: Eyre and Spottiswoode, 1886.

FITCH, SIR JOSHUA. *Thomas and Matthew Arnold and Their Influence on English Education*. New York: Charles Scribner's Sons, 1897.

General Statues, 19th and 20th Years of Queen Victoria. London, 1856.

GUTHRIE, WILLIAM BELL. *Matthew Arnold's Diaries: The Unpublished Items*. Ann Arbor: University Microfilms, 1959.

HANSARD, T.C. *The Parliamentary Debates from the Year 1801 to the Present Time*. Vol. XXXIV. London: Longman, Hurst, Rees, Orme, and Brown, *et al.*

———— *The Parliamentary Debates*, New Series, Commencing with the Accession of George IV. London: Baldwin, *et al.*

———— *Hansard's Parliamentary Debates*, Third Series. London: T. C. Hansard.

HARDING, FRANK J.W. *Matthew Arnold, the Critic, and France.* Genève: Librairie Droz, 1964.

HIPPLE, WALTER J., JR. "Matthew Arnold, Dialectician." *University of Toronto Quarterly* XXXII (October 1962): 1–26.

HUXLEY, THOMAS HENRY. "A Liberal Education and Where to Find It." In *Collected Essays*, vol. III. New York and London: D. Appleton and Co., 1917.

JOHNSON, SAMUEL. *The Six Chief Lives from Johnson's "Lives of the Poets."* Edited by Matthew Arnold. London: Macmillan and Co., 1881.

KAY-SHUTTLEWORTH, SIR JAMES. *Four Periods of Public Education as*

Reviewed in 1832, 1839, 1846, and 1862. London: Longman, Green, Longman, and Roberts, 1862.

———— "Letter to Earl Granville, K.G., on the Revised Code of Regulations Contained in the Minute of the Committee of Council on Education Dated July 29th, 1861." In *Four Periods of Public Education.* London: Longman, Green, Longman, and Roberts, 1862.

———— *Public Education as Affected by the Minutes of the Committee of the Privy Council from 1846 to 1852.* London: Longman, Brown, Green, and Longmans, 1853.

LANCASTER, JOSEPH. *Improvements in Education, as It Respects the Industrious Classes.* 3d ed. with additions. London: Darton and Harvey, 1805.

LOWNDES, G.A.N. *The Silent Social Revolution.* London: Oxford University Press, 1937.

LOWRY, HOWARD FOSTER. *The Letters of Matthew Arnold to Arthur Hugh Clough.* London and New York: Oxford University Press, 1932.

MCCARTHY, PATRICK J. *Matthew Arnold and the Three Classes.* New York: Columbia University Press, 1964.

MACK, EDWARD CLARENCE. *Public Schools and British Opinion since 1860.* New York: Columbia University Press, 1941.

MEIKLEJOHN, ALEXANDER. *Education between Two Worlds.* New York: Harper and Brothers, 1942.

MILL, JOHN STUART. *The Autobiography of John Stuart Mill.* New York: Columbia University Press, 1944.

———— *On Liberty and Other Essays.* New York: The Book League of America, 1929.

MONTMORENCY, JAMES EDWARD G., DE. *The Progress of Education in England.* London: Knight and Co., 1904.

NEIMAN, FRASER. *Essays, Letters, and Reviews by Matthew Arnold.* Cambridge: Harvard University Press, 1960.

———— "The Zeitgeist of Matthew Arnold." *PMLA* LXXII (December 1957): 977–96.

REID, T. WEMYSS. *Life of the Right Honourable William Forster.* London: Chapman and Hall, Ltd., 1888.

Reports of the Assistant Commissioners Appointed to Inquire into the State of Popular Education in Continental Europe and on Educational Charities in England and Wales. Vol. IV. London: Eyre and Spottiswoode, 1861.

Reports of the Commissioners Appointed to Inquire into the State of Popular Education in England (The Duke of Newcastle Commission). 6 vols. London: Eyre and Spottiswoode, 1861.

SENIOR, NASSAU W. *Suggestions on Popular Education.* London: John Murray, 1861.

SNEYD-KYNNERSLEY, EDMUND MACKENZIE. *H. M. I. Some Passages in the Life of One of H. M. Inspectors of Schools.* London: Macmillan and Co., Ltd., 1908.

TAYLOR, A.C. *Carlyle et la pensée latine.* Paris: Ancienne Librairie Furne, 1937.

TILLOTSON, KATHLEEN MARY. "Matthew Arnold and Carlyle." (Warton Lecture on English Poetry). *Proceedings of the British Academy,* London: Oxford University Press, 1956.

TRILLING, LIONEL. *Matthew Arnold.* New York: W. W. Norton and Co., 1939.

WALPOLE, SIR SPENCER. *A History of England from the Conclusion of the Great War in 1815.* 5 vols. London: Longsmans, Green and Co., 1886.

INDEX

This book
was designed by
WILLIAM RUETER
under the direction of
ALLAN FLEMING
and was printed by
University of
Toronto
Press